Beauty by
The Book *for Teens*

Becoming a Biblically Beautiful Young Woman

A 7-Week Study of Proverbs

Laurie Cole

Author & Teacher

Production Coordinator • Pam Henderson
Cover and Layout Design • Debbie Todd
Graphic Design • Julie Riley, j.riley creative LLC
Editorial Team • Emily Ryan and Hannah Mahanay
Photography • Don & Mary Carico, Lakewood Photography, League City, TX

Priority Ministries
Encouraging Women to Give God Glory & Priority

www.priorityministries.org

Dedication

To Juliette,
my precious granddaughter.
I love you to pieces.

Acknowledgements

Priority Ministries was privileged and blessed to pilot *Beauty by The Book for Teens* in 2010 with a fantastic group of teenage girls from **Sagemont Church in Houston, Texas**, and their leaders, **Scott Condict**, Minister to Students, and **Ruth Birdsong**, Minister to Girls.

Each week of the pilot, the girls completed their *Beauty by The Book for Teens* homework, participated in small groups, and met with Laurie for a teaching session. And each and every week, they graciously and patiently filled out evaluation forms providing us with invaluable insights which enabled us to revise and improve the study you now hold in your hands. We thank the Lord for each and every girl who participated in the pilot, for their leaders, and for the tremendous blessing they've been to us and, ultimately, to you.

We also want to recognize and express our love and gratitude to **Wanda Shellenbarger**, Women's and Girl's Ministry Director, First Baptist Church Carl Junction, Missouri, whose encouragement, example, and prayer support was absolutely key in the development of *Beauty by The Book for Teens*. Thank you, Wanda, for your heart to reach and teach God's Word to teenage girls. We are especially grateful for your love for the girls in the Missouri Baptist Children's Homes. God used your example and the precious testimonies of the girls you taught there to inspire us to step out by faith and produce *Beauty by The Book for Teens*, our very first Bible study for girls.

"I thank my God in all my remembrance of you."
Philippians 1:3 *NAS*

About the Study

This Bible study is a simple tool to help you discover life-changing truths from God's Word. Think of this workbook as a chisel and your Bible as a gold mine. Each day you'll "dig-in" to God's Word to discover precious treasures that will enrich your life for His glory (Psalm 19:9–10, 119:162). Homework for this study will require approximately 20 minutes per day, five days per week.

The Holy Spirit will be your Divine Tutor throughout this study (John 16:13), and prayer will be essential in facilitating your sensitivity to His leadership. Therefore, a *pray* paragraph is included at the beginning of each day's homework. At the conclusion of your daily study, you'll be encouraged to record any insights the Holy Spirit has shown you in a brief *reflect* section.

A good translation of the Bible will be essential as you use this study. The *New Living Translation*, Second Edition, the *New International Version*, the *New American Standard Bible*, the *New King James Version*, or the *King James Version* are all very accurate translations and are highly recommended. In this study, the author will primarily use the *New Living Translation*.

Also included in this workbook are seven Listening Guides. These fill-in-the-blank guides are designed to be used with the *Beauty by The Book for Teens* downloadable videos, DVD or CD sets which include seven teaching sessions with Laurie Cole (approximately 25–30 minutes per session). The *Beauty by The Book for Teens* downloadable videos, DVD or CD sets are recommended but are optional. For more information about these resources, please visit www.priorityministries.com/shop.

About the Author

Laurie Cole is the Founder and President of Priority Ministries, a ministry dedicated to encouraging and equipping women to love God most and seek Him first. Raised in a strong Christian home, Laurie became a Christian at an early age. But in her early twenties, God tested and taught her the importance of truly giving Him priority in her life.

In 1985, Laurie enrolled in an in-depth women's Bible study. Encouraged by the older women who led the study, Laurie received training and began teaching and leading a group where God affirmed His call upon her life to teach. For over 20 years, Laurie has taught dozens of Bible studies, spoken at numerous women's events and conferences, and is the author of three in-depth Bible studies: *There Is A Season*, *The Temple*, and *Beauty by The Book*. Her passion for God and hunger for His Word continues to grow.

A minister's wife, Laurie and her husband, Bill, serve the Lord at Sagemont Church in Houston, Texas, where he is the Associate Pastor of Worship and Praise. They have been married for 32 years and have three sons (David, Kevin, and J.J.), one beloved daughter-in-law (Stephanie), and two glorious grandchildren (Ezra and Juliette).

Table of Contents

Beauty by The Book for Teens *Workbook*

Beauty by The Book for Teens *Teacher Guide*   129

Introduction to the Study

I am absolutely overjoyed that you are holding this book in your hands! You see, I never intended to write a Bible study specifically targeted at teens, but God had other plans—and those plans included you. Let me explain.

A few years ago, I wrote and released *Beauty by The Book* for the same group of women I've pretty much always written for and taught: adult women. Women 21 and older. But right after those women started doing the study, something very unexpected happened. Those women began asking me about you. They'd say things like:

"This study has taught me how to become a godly woman.
Now I can't wait to teach it to my girls small group.
Do you have a Beauty by The Book *workbook just for teens?"*

"I can't wait to do this study with my teen-age daughter.
I want her to learn these truths while she's young. I sure wish I had."

"My life would have been radically different if someone had taught me
these principles when I was a teenager. I hope one day you'll write a
Beauty by The Book Bible *study for young women. They really need it."*

My response to women who told me things like that was always, "Thanks for the encouragement. I'll pray about it." So I did. I prayed, and prayed, and prayed, until God showed me very clearly that you had always been part of His plan for this study. What a delightful surprise that was to me!

But there's another reason why writing this study for you is such a surprise to me. As the mother of three sons, I have never enjoyed the privilege of raising girls or of teaching a daughter how to become a godly woman—and I didn't think I ever would. But God always knew about you. What a gift it is to study and share His Word with you, precious you.

In today's culture, beauty is an idol worshipped and pursued by multitudes of women both young and old. Biblical beauty, however, is vastly different from worldly beauty—but you probably already know that. What you may not know, however, is just how much you have been influenced by the world's definition and beliefs about beauty. Therefore, before you even begin this study, I must warn you: Pursuing biblical beauty will require you to swim against some very strong cultural currents. But you can do it!

Like the constantly changing hemlines of today's fashions, the world's definition of beauty will continually evolve. But one thing will never change: God's Word—The Book. More relevant today than the latest issue of *Seventeen*. More liberating than the most recent reinvention of feminism. God's Word is timeless, transformational, and true. Study its standards, practice its principles and you will become a true beauty—a biblically beautiful young woman of God.

Your Sister,

Laurie

> "The grass withers, and the flowers fade,
> but the Word of our God stands forever."
> —Isaiah 40:8 *NLT*

Introductory Week • *Physical Beauty vs. Biblical Beauty*

Physical Beauty...

1) Is *God-Given*. *Ezekiel 28:12*

2) Is *attention-getting*. *Ezekiel 28:13–14*

3) Is *pride-inducing*. *Ezekiel 28:17*

4) Is *spiritually corrupting*. *Ezekiel 28:16–17*

Biblical Beauty...

1) Is *God-Given*. *1 Peter 3:4*

2) Is *gentle* and *quiet*. *1 Peter 3:4*

3) Is *precious* in God's sight. *1 Peter 3:4*

4) Is *unfading* and *eternal*. *1 Peter 3:4*

Question: How can you become a biblically beautiful young woman?

Answer: By *beholding* God and *upholding* the standard of His Word.

Week 1 • *Five Beauty Dos & Don'ts*

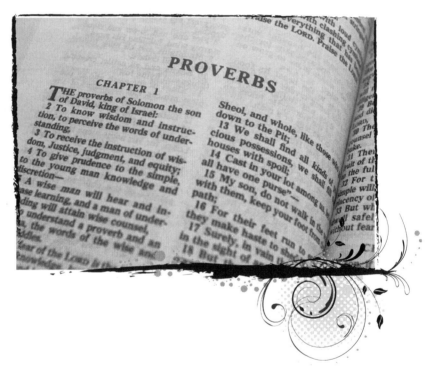

This week, I will be introducing you to five women. These five females all make their home in the Book of Proverbs. For the next six weeks, we will be spending quite a bit of time with them as we learn how to become biblically beautiful. But before you meet them, you need to know something: not all of these women qualify as true biblical beauties.

Let me explain. You've probably seen those "beauty do" and "beauty don't" photos in the fashion magazines haven't you? Well, some of the five women you're about to meet are biblical "beauty dos," but others are biblical "beauty don'ts." And trust me, you won't have any trouble telling which ones are which.

So, c'mon. Let's head to Proverbs—our home for the next six weeks.

Day One

I almost forgot to tell you, there is a sixth "woman" we'll be getting to know in Proverbs. Her name is Wisdom. All throughout Proverbs, the author uses the female pronoun "she" to refer to wisdom. Don't you just love that! But let's not get too carried away, because there is a seventh "woman" mentioned in the Proverbs, and her name is Folly.

This sixth "woman"—Wisdom—will be the focus of our daily *pray* time. If you want to become a biblically beautiful young woman, it is essential that you get to know Ms. Wisdom well.

pray

1. Good news! Wisdom is available to everyone who needs it, and we *all* need it. James 1:5 promises that "if any of you lack wisdom, let him ask of God who gives to all men generously and without reproach and it will be given to him" (*NASB*). Begin your first day of study by bowing your head and praising God as the source of true wisdom. Ask Him to pour out His wisdom upon you and make you wise.

> *Wisdom shouts in the streets.*
> *She cries out in the public square…*
> *"Come here and listen to me!*
> *I'll pour out the spirit of wisdom*
> *upon you and make you wise."*
> —Proverbs 1:20–23

2. Brace yourself. You're about to meet Beauty #1, the first female mentioned in Proverbs, and she's a doozy. Allow me to introduce you to the **Immoral Woman** as you read Proverbs 5:3–6:

> ³ *For the lips of an adulteress [woman] drip honey,*
>   *and her speech is smoother than oil;*
> ⁴ *but in the end she is bitter as gall,*
>   *sharp as a double edged sword.*
> ⁵ *Her feet go down to death;*
>   *her steps lead straight to the grave.*
> ⁶ *She gives no thought to the way of life;*
>   *her paths are crooked, but she knows it not.*
>   —Proverbs 5:3–6 *NIV*

3. Based upon Proverbs 5:3–6, please answer the following questions about the Immoral Woman:

   a. What's the very first thing you learned about her, and what kind of first impression does she usually make (verse 3)?

   > At first, the Immoral Woman may appear sweet since that's how Proverbs 5:3 describes her words. They "drip honey, and her speech is smoother than oil."

   b. According to verse 4, what will others eventually discover about her, and when will they discover it?

   > Others will eventually discover that she's bitter not sweet, sharp and destructive not smooth — the exact opposite of what she first appeared to be.

   c. What is her final destination and why (verses 5–6)?

   > Her final destination is death because she gives no thought or consideration to choosing the path that leads to life (God's path). Her path — her choices and her way of life — is crooked and dangerous, but she does not know it.

   You've just experienced your first encounter with the Immoral Woman, but it won't be your last. Next week, you'll study her extensively, and you may be surprised to learn that five passages and one entire chapter of Proverbs are devoted to her. She gets more press and attention than any of the other four women we'll be studying, and she certainly gets the most press in today's world, which leads me to ask this:

4. If you had to name the top three places you most consistently see the Immoral Woman in our culture, where would they be? For example: on television.

   > Possible answers include:
   > - on the covers of popular magazines
   > - in the fashion industry
   > - in movies
   > - in music videos, MTV, and in the popular music industry
   > - on television and in many popular television programs
   > - in commercials for just about everything
   > - online everywhere
   > - on outdoor billboards

5. Why do you think five passages and one entire chapter of Proverbs are devoted to the Immoral Woman? In other words, why would God want us to get to know her so well?

> God knows that the Immoral Woman is very popular today, and that her influence in our culture is deep. Throngs of girls and women emulate her. But God wants us to be able to recognize the Immoral Woman for who she really is: a dangerous and destructive role model. He loves us, and He desires His very best for us. And because He does, He wants to warn and protect us from following her crooked path.

6. A few minutes ago, you prayed and asked God for wisdom. What wisdom has He given you through your study today?

reflect

> Personal application; answers will vary.

Day Two

pray

1. Tuning into God has never been more difficult than it is today. Hearing His still, small voice over the nonstop noise of technology—ringing cell phones, texting alerts, and 24/7 access to the internet—is no small feat. But by daily and deliberately making today's Proverb a priority, you can still hear God speak. So, right now, tune out the racket around you, and tune in to God and His wisdom through prayer.

> *Tune your ears to wisdom, and*
> *concentrate on understanding.*
> —Proverbs 2:2

Today you will meet two more women from Proverbs: the Indiscreet Woman and the Irritating Woman. I know. They probably don't sound like the kind of women who can teach us much about biblical beauty, but here's a great passage to remind us why we can't afford to ignore them:

All Scripture is inspired by God and is useful to teach us what is true
and to make us realize what is wrong in our lives. It straightens us out
and teaches us to do what is right. It is God's way of preparing us in every way,
fully equipped for every good thing God wants us to do.
—2 Timothy 3:16–17

2. Keeping 2 Timothy 3:16–17 in mind, meet Beauty #2 by reading the following scripture:

A woman who is beautiful but lacks discretion
is like a gold ring in a pig's snout.
— Proverbs 11:22

Wow! That's one blunt verse, huh? While Beauty #2, the **Indiscreet Woman**, may be rich in the looks department, her lack of discretion is her ruin. Thus, one of the primary principles we can learn from her is that no amount of make-up, spa treatments, Botox® injections, or even plastic surgery can cover up a deficit of discretion.

So what exactly is discretion? To answer that question, find and circle the synonyms of discretion hidden in the Word Search puzzle.

Synonyms of Discretion

S	F	U	S	U	I	A	L	B	S	J	N	Y	P	G	N	I
B	N	N	R	V	X	W	U	Y	S	E	I	K	X	J	O	O
F	O	D	K	G	R	B	I	B	G	X	J	X	O	H	I	E
J	S	E	L	O	C	D	I	S	C	E	R	N	M	E	N	T
I	U	R	J	O	K	V	S	F	D	M	O	O	K	Z	U	K
Z	F	S	A	D	U	N	P	X	P	O	D	X	K	T	B	K
V	F	T	U	T	E	W	E	B	N	H	M	P	J	R	E	N
L	K	A	M	A	S	E	R	Y	G	D	U	D	E	F	S	O
G	C	N	L	S	B	K	H	G	C	P	H	N	P	Z	V	W
O	F	D	U	T	S	S	E	L	F	C	O	N	T	R	O	L
O	N	I	W	E	T	M	D	C	C	N	C	L	F	B	U	E
D	S	N	K	Q	T	A	C	P	S	C	E	E	F	R	Z	D
S	D	G	O	O	D	J	U	D	G	M	E	N	T	J	U	G
E	C	L	F	B	F	U	S	K	I	R	Q	T	A	C	T	E
N	C	E	E	F	R	Z	D	Q	M	R	J	B	A	H	Y	L
S	S	C	L	I	N	T	E	L	L	I	G	E	N	C	E	A
E	O	J	L	H	T	R	A	F	Y	Z	Z	X	T	K	B	C

Wisdom	Discernment	Understanding
Knowledge	Intelligence	Self-control
Good judgment	Good sense	Good taste

3. After seeing those synonyms, it's pretty obvious, huh? Discretion is a must-have for every biblically beautiful young woman. In a couple of weeks, we'll study discretion in detail. But for now, discover how you can get discretion by picking up your Bible, reading Proverbs 1:1–5, and answering the following questions:

a. Who wrote the Book of Proverbs?

> Solomon, the son of David, king of Israel (v. 1).

b. Why did he write it (verses 2–5)?

> Proverbs 1:2-5
> ² "Their purpose is to teach people wisdom and discipline, to help them understand the insights of the wise. ³ Their purpose is to teach people to live disciplined and successful lives, to help them do what is right, just, and fair. ⁴ These proverbs will give insight to the simple, knowledge and discernment to the young. ⁵ Let the wise listen to these proverbs and become even wiser. Let those with understanding receive guidance."

c. According to this passage, how can we obtain discretion?

> We can obtain discretion by studying and applying God's Word and, specifically, the Book of Proverbs. It teaches how to live "disciplined and successful lives" (v. 3), and it helps us "do what is right, just, and fair" (v. 3). And studying Proverbs will give "knowledge and discernment to [even] the young" (v. 4).

Let's move along for now and meet Beauty #3, the **Irritating Woman**. We won't spend much time with her today, but that's okay, because a little time with her goes a long way!

4. Meet Beauty #3 by reading the following scriptures:

    NOTE: The word "contentious" means argumentative and quarrelsome.[1]

    > *It is better to live alone in the corner of an attic*
    > *than with a contentious wife in a lovely home.*
    > —Proverbs 21:9

    > *It is better to live alone in the desert*
    > *than with a crabby complaining wife.*
    > — Proverbs 21:19

    We've all met women like this before haven't we? But let's be honest: at times, we've all been her, too. And while these verses may apply to women, you and I both know that crabbiness does not discriminate. Anyone (young or old, male or female, single or married, Christian or non-Christian) can exhibit the classic symptoms of what I call "3C Syndrome": (1) Contentiousness, (2) Crabbiness, with frequent bouts of (3) Complaining.

    Fortunately, 3C is not generally contagious, and there is a cure (we'll uncover it in the weeks ahead). But for now, let's focus on the primary and possible long-term effects of 3C.

5. According to Proverbs 21:9 and 19:

    a. How does 3C affect our relationships with others?

    > • It causes others to dread and/or not want to spend time with us.
    > • It pushes people away from us, even those we like, enjoy, and love.

    b. What potential long-term effects could 3C cause in our relationships with others?

    > • 3C strains our relationships with others and takes a negative, toxic toll upon our life and theirs.
    > • 3C may cause others to choose to reject having a relationship with us altogether.
    > • 3C women will very likely become very lonely women.

6. Might *you* have a mild (or possibly serious) case of 3C? Take a quick check-up by circling the word that most accurately completes each of the following sentences:

> Personal application; answers will vary.

   a. My friends and family would probably say that I am crabby:

      rarely   occasionally   frequently

   b. My friends and family would probably say that I complain:

      rarely   occasionally   frequently

   c. My friends and family would probably say that I am usually:

      easygoing   a little high-maintenance   downright difficult

   d. My friends and family would probably say that my words are usually:

      encouraging and kind   sweet and sour   negative and nagging

7. If your check-up revealed a possible case of 3C, a quick dose of wisdom and instruction from Proverbs should ease some of your symptoms until we can study the cure in the weeks ahead. Begin applying the following verses to your life as often and as liberally as needed:

> *Don't talk too much, for it fosters sin.*
> *Be sensible and turn off the flow!*
> —Proverbs 10:19

> *Kind words are like honey—*
> *Sweet to the soul and healthy for the body.*
> —Proverbs 16:24

8. Do you agree that there is a lot we can learn from the two women we've met today? What insights has the Holy Spirit taught you today through the Indiscreet Woman and the Irritating Woman?

reflect

> Personal application; answers will vary.
> _____
> _____
> _____
> _____

Day Three

pray

1. The fear of the Lord is a very positive and beneficial thing. It is where true wisdom begins. So what exactly is it? Very simply, the fear of the Lord is reverence (deep respect and awe[2]) for God that results in obedience to God. It is both attitude (reverence) and action (obedience); and when you put them together, you get wisdom! Before you begin today's study, submit yourself in reverence before God in prayer, and commit to obey Him. Then watch for wisdom to show up.

*Fear of the LORD
is the beginning of wisdom.
Knowledge of the Holy One
results in understanding.*
—Proverbs 9:10

2. I am very excited today to introduce you to Beauty #4. This woman bears no resemblance to the three women you have previously met in Proverbs—thank goodness! So, without further adieu, it is my privilege to introduce you now to Beauty #4, the **Captivating Woman**:

> [18] *Let your wife be a fountain of blessing for you.
> Rejoice in the wife of your youth.*
> [19] *She is a loving doe, a graceful deer.
> Let her breasts satisfy you always.
> May you always be captivated by her love.*
> —Proverbs 5:18–19

Every scripture in the Bible is inspired by God. He is the ultimate Author of every passage and verse (2 Peter 1:21). Therefore, when you read a sensual passage like Proverbs 5:18–19, you need to remember that God Himself wrote it. So it's pretty obvious to see that when it comes to sex, God is no prude. But to more fully understand God's view about sex, you need to take a second look at Proverbs 5:18–19.

3. Circle the correct answer to each of the following questions:

    a. According to Proverbs 5:18–19, who is God encouraging to enjoy sex?

    Any man | A husband |

    b. According to Proverbs 5:18–19, who is the captivating woman?

    Any woman | A wife |

    c. According to Proverbs 5:18–19, who is God instructing and encouraging to enjoy sexual intimacy?

    Any relationship | A married couple |

The first seven chapters of Proverbs are specifically addressed from a father (Solomon, the author of Proverbs) to his son. In Proverbs 5:18–19, the father is exhorting his son to seek love and sexual satisfaction within the bounds of a monogamous marriage to a Captivating Woman.

But Proverbs 5:18–19 has a message for women, too. I believe it teaches women—married women—to be sensually, sexually satisfying wives. So as an unmarried teenager, how does this passage apply to you? I believe God's message to you is this: When you become a wife, you should become a Captivating Woman…but not until then.

4. From the beginning, God designed and reserved sex for marriage. See it for yourself by opening your Bible and reading Genesis 2:21–25. It's the beautiful account of the very first bride and the very first wedding (and note in verse 22 who gives the bride away—so amazing!). After you've read this passage, write out verses 24–25 word-for-word.

> Although students will only be writing out verses 24-25, the entire passage is below.
> Genesis 2:21-25
> [21] "So the LORD God caused the man to fall into a deep sleep. While the man slept, the LORD God took out one of the man's ribs and closed up the opening. [22] Then the LORD God made a woman from the rib, and he brought her to the man. [23] 'At last!' the man exclaimed. 'This one is bone from my bone, and flesh from my flesh! She will be called 'woman,' because she was taken from 'man.' [24] **This explains why a man leaves his father and mother and is joined to his wife, and the two are united into one. [25] Now the man and his wife were both naked, but they felt no shame.**"

5. How does Genesis 2:21-25 parallel Proverbs 5:18–19?

> - Both passages teach that God reserves sex for marriage between a husband and wife.
> - Both passages reveal that God designed sex within marriage as something good and enjoyable.
> - In Gen. 2, Adam and Eve were "both naked, but they felt no shame" (v. 25). This parallels the purity and shamelessness of sex between a husband and wife in Prov. 5.
> - Adam's joy in Eve (Gen. 2:23) parallels God's command (Prov. 5:15) that husbands "rejoice" in their wives.

6. Describe the conflict you see between our culture's view of sex and the biblical view of sex.

> - The Bible reserves sex for marriage, but the culture condones it outside the bonds of marriage.
> - The Bible encourages husbands and wives to enjoy sexuality, but the culture encourages unmarried people to enjoy and experiment with sex before marriage.

7. As a young woman, how has God spoken to your heart through His Word today?

reflect

> Personal application; answers will vary.
> _____
> _____
> _____
> _____

Day Four

1. What's at the top of your "want list"? You know what I mean—most of us have a list in our head of things we'd really like to have. But do you know what should always be at the very top? Wisdom. Take today's passage before the Lord in prayer, and commit to giving it priority on your "want list."

> *Choose (wisdom's) instruction rather than silver,*
> *and knowledge over pure gold.*
> *For wisdom is far more valuable than rubies.*
> *Nothing you desire can be compared with it.*
> —Proverbs 8:10–11

2. Thus far, you've met the first four women from Proverbs. Are you ready to meet our final beauty, Beauty #5? You may have heard about her before. Hands down, she's the most well-known woman in Proverbs. Prepare to be dazzled as you meet Beauty #5: the **Ideal Woman**.

Proverbs 31:10–31

10 *Who can find a virtuous and capable wife? She is worth more than precious rubies.*
11 *Her husband can trust her, and she will greatly enrich his life.*
12 *She will not hinder him but help him all her life.*
13 *She finds wool and flax and busily spins it.*
14 *She is like a merchant's ship; she brings her food from afar.*
15 *She gets up before dawn to prepare breakfast for her household and plan the day's work for her servant girls.*
16 *She goes out to inspect a field and buys it; with her earnings she plants a vineyard.*
17 *She is energetic and strong, a hard worker.*
18 *She watches for bargains; her lights burn late into the night.*
19 *Her hands are busy spinning thread, her fingers twisting fiber.*
20 *She extends a helping hand to the poor and opens her arms to the needy.*
21 *She has no fear of winter for her household because all of them have warm clothes.*
22 *She quilts her own bedspreads. She dresses like royalty in gowns of finest cloth.*
23 *Her husband is well known, for he sits in the council meeting with the other civic leaders.*

²⁴ She makes belted linen garments and sashes to sell to the merchants.
²⁵ She is clothed with strength and dignity, and she laughs with no fear of the future.
²⁶ When she speaks, her words are wise, and kindness is the rule when she gives instructions.
²⁷ She carefully watches all that goes on in her household and does not have to bear the consequences of laziness.
²⁸ Her children stand and bless her. Her husband praises her:
²⁹ "There are many virtuous and capable women in the world, but you surpass them all!"
³⁰ Charm is deceptive, and beauty does not last; but a woman who fears the LORD will be greatly praised.
³¹ Reward her for all she has done. Let her deeds publicly declare her praise.

After reading such an extensive passage extolling the virtues of the Ideal Woman, the phrase "total package" comes to my mind. Wow! This woman's got it all and, furthermore, she's got it all *very* together.

But don't get the idea that this passage is describing a typical day-in-the-life-of the Ideal Woman. No one can do everything mentioned in this passage in a single day. Instead, Proverbs 31:10-31 paints a panoramic picture for us of the Ideal Women's life, character, and career as a wife, mother, entrepreneur, and servant of God. Here we see samples of the seasons of a woman's life. But we also see something else: a role model for women young and old.

3. As you read Proverbs 31:10–31, which of the Ideal Woman's qualities, characteristics, and accomplishments do you most desire for your own life?

> Personal application; many possible answers.

4. Prepare today to become an Ideal Woman someday. Find out how by reading 1 Timothy 4:12, underlining it in your Bible, and writing it out word-for-word below.

> (NLT) " Don't let anyone think less of you because you are young. Be an example to all believers in what you say, in the way you live, in your love, your faith, and your purity."

5. How has God spoken to your heart through His Word today?

reflect

Personal application; answers will vary.

Day Five

pray

1. The Book of Proverbs is a collection of wise sayings written and edited by Solomon to teach us how to live wise, godly lives (Proverbs 1:1–6). The benefits of wise living are obvious in the following Proverb. As you conclude the first week of your study, pray and thank God for the wisdom you've already gleaned and for the benefits you've already seen.

Wisdom
will multiply your days
and add years to your life.
*If you become **wise**,*
you will be the one to benefit.
*If you scorn **wisdom**,*
you will be the one to suffer.
—Proverbs 9:11–12

This week, you've briefly met the five females from Proverbs. In the next five weeks, these women will teach us the basics of biblical beauty. But before we conclude this first week of study, there's one very important thing we must do: we need to define biblical beauty.

The first thing you need to know is that biblical beauty is very different from physical beauty, the kind of beauty our world worships. Every single day, girls are bombarded with images of the world's definition of beauty: perfect hair, perfect clothes and (above all) the perfect shape, size, and weight. The result? Millions of girls strive to attain that standard, and many of them end up struggling with poor self-image, eating disorders, depression, and other forms of self-destructive behavior.

But is the world's definition of beauty true? To answer that question, you need to go to the very source of truth: God's Word. In fact, Jesus affirmed that God's Word is true ("Thy word is truth." John 17:17). So, pick up your copy of The Truth—your Bible—and begin your final day of study this week as you discover the real truth about beauty and how God defines it.

2. According to the following passages, what do you learn about biblical beauty? Record your answers in the space provided.

    a. 1 Samuel 16:7

> *(NLT)* "But the LORD said to Samuel, 'Don't judge by his appearance or height, for I have rejected him. The LORD doesn't see things the way you see them. People judge by outward appearance, but the LORD looks at the heart.'"
>
> There are two types of beauty: outward and inward. God sees and values inward beauty. Biblical beauty comes from the inside out, and it is the result of a beautiful heart.

    b. 1 Peter 3:3–4

> *(NLT)* [3] "Don't be concerned about the outward beauty of fancy hairstyles, expensive jewelry, or beautiful clothes. [4] You should clothe yourselves instead with the beauty that comes from within, the unfading beauty of a gentle and quiet spirit, which is so precious to God."
>
> Biblical beauty should be our primary goal. It comes from within our hearts, and it is greatly valued by God.

3. The prophet Isaiah foretold Christ's coming in great detail. He even provided us with information about Jesus' physical appearance and beauty. Read Isaiah 53:2, and record what you learn about the beauty of Christ.

NOTE: the "servant" in this verse refers to Christ.

> *(NLT)* "My servant grew up in the LORD's presence like a tender green shoot, like a root in dry ground. There was nothing beautiful or majestic about his appearance, nothing to attract us to him."
>
> Jesus was not physically beautiful. His outward appearance was not the reason others were attracted to Him.

4. Using all of the scriptural information you acquired in Questions 2 and 3, define biblical beauty in your own words by completing the following sentence:

Biblical beauty is…

> Answers will vary but may include the following:
>
> Biblical beauty is very different from physical beauty. Physical beauty is outward; biblical beauty is inward. Although God alone can see the heart, the outward evidences of biblical beauty are purity, good character, wisdom, and a gentle, quiet spirit.

5. Based upon everything you've studied this week about biblical beauty, check the box that correctly describes each of our 5 Beauties from the Proverbs:

   a. The Immoral Woman is a:
   - ☐ Biblical Beauty Do
   - ☑ **Biblical Beauty Don't**

   b. The Indiscreet Woman is a:
   - ☐ Biblical Beauty Do
   - ☑ **Biblical Beauty Don't**

   c. The Irritating Woman is a:
   - ☐ Biblical Beauty Do
   - ☑ **Biblical Beauty Don't**

   d. The Captivating Woman is a:
   - ☑ **Biblical Beauty Do**
   - ☐ Biblical Beauty Don't

   e. The Ideal Woman is a:
   - ☑ **Biblical Beauty Do**
   - ☐ Biblical Beauty Don't

6. Be honest. Be real. How has the world's definition of beauty affected you?

> Personal application; answers will vary.

7. Now, think about this: How will pursuing biblical beauty affect you?

> Personal application; answers will vary.

8. It's time to make a choice, precious girl. What kind of beauty will you choose to pursue? Please circle one:

> Personal application; answers will vary.

Physical Beauty   Biblical Beauty

9. You've had a great week of study. You've saturated your heart with God's Word, and you've given Him an opportunity to speak truth into your life. So, as you reflect upon all that you've learned and studied, what has the Lord most impressed upon your heart and life?

reflect

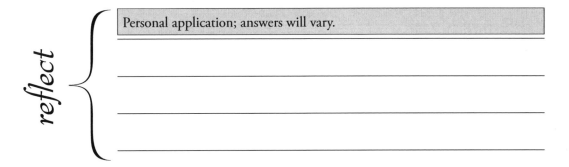

> Personal application; answers will vary.

On June 14, 2007, a well-known biblical beauty died. After many years of declining health, Ruth Bell Graham (wife of evangelist Billy Graham) went to be with the Lord at the age of 87. At her funeral, her children remembered her as funny, feisty, and full of love for Jesus and His Word.

Although he was not expected nor scheduled to speak, Billy Graham rose spontaneously to his feet and spoke at Ruth's service. In his brief address, he recalled the previous evening when he'd visited the funeral home to see Ruth one last time. Then he said, "I wish you could look into the casket because she's so beautiful." Ruth's beauty transcended even death.

In a world that worships physical, temporal beauty, the life and death of Ruth Bell Graham proves that biblical beauty is timeless and eternal. It has the awesome power to grow and intensify even as our bodies weaken and fade. It is the amazing promise to all who love the Lord and live His Word. It is real beauty. It is rare beauty. It is beauty by The Book.

NOTE: Find out more about Ruth Graham's childhood, teen-age, and adult life by reading her biography, *Ruth: A Portrait, The Story of Ruth Bell Graham*, by Patricia Cornwell. You'll love it!

Week One • *Biblical Beauty According to Proverbs*

Background on Proverbs:

1) *Author of Proverbs:* <u>Solomon</u> Proverbs 1:1

2) *Purpose of Proverbs* (1:2–6): To give wisdom, discipline, understanding, prudence, knowledge and discretion to the <u>*wise*</u> AND the <u>*unwise*</u>.

3) *Primary Principle of Proverbs* (1:7): The fear of the Lord is the <u>*beginning / foundation*</u> of wisdom and knowledge.
   The fear of the Lord = <u>Reverence</u> for God
   that results in <u>*obedience*</u> to God.

4) *Present Day Proverb:*
   <u>"You gotta know better to do better."</u>
   Our Goal as we study Proverbs: To <u>*know*</u> AND
   <u>*do / obey*</u> **God better.**

Biblical Beauty Dos: According to Proverbs:

1) <u>*Pure*</u> and <u>*modest*</u>. (Beauty Don't #1: The Immoral Woman)

2) <u>*Wise*</u> and <u>*discreet*</u>. (Beauty Don't #2: The Indiscreet Woman)

3) <u>*Edifying*</u> and <u>*encouraging*</u>. (Beauty Don't #3: The Irritating Woman)

4) <u>*Fascinating*</u> and <u>*attractive*</u>. (Beauty Do #1: The Captivating Woman)

5) <u>*Strong*</u> and <u>*spiritual*</u>. (Beauty Do #2: The Ideal Woman)

Week 2 • *The Immoral Woman*

   Teen hotties. Visit any mall in America and you'll spot them sporting skintight t-shirts and jeans, baring their cleavage proudly, and shopping for lingerie with their boyfriends in Victoria's Secret. As far as the culture is concerned, none of this is a big deal. But what about God? Is He concerned about teen hotties? Absolutely, but it might surprise you to know that He's not one bit shocked by them either.

So who is this hottie our culture craves and adores? The Bible calls her the Immoral Woman and guess what? She wants you to become her friend…and her follower. But beware, because this is where her friendship will ultimately lead you: "The lips of an immoral woman are as sweet as honey…[but] her steps lead straight to the grave" (Proverbs 5:3–5). Make no mistake, the Immoral Woman is a sweet-talking, back-stabbing, satanic strategist, and she's hell-bent on one thing: destroying you.

Girl, it's time to rise up and declare war on the Immoral Woman. But there's only one way to defeat her: you must arm yourself with the truth of God's Word—it's kryptonite to every satanic power including her. So study well this week, because victory is yours for the taking.

> *You are from God, little children, and have overcome them;*
> *because greater is He who is in you than he who is in the world.*
> —1 John 4:4 *NASB*

Day One

pray

1. Begin your study this week in prayer by asking God to search your heart and reveal all the impurities in your life. Be still. Allow God to speak to you. Take time to confess each sin to Him, and receive His cleansing and forgiveness. Commit to complete repentance, and ask God for wisdom to keep you pure.

> *Wisdom will save you from the immoral woman,*
> *from the flattery of the adulterous woman.*
> —Proverbs 2:16

The Immoral Woman has become so popular these days that some people don't even recognize her for the heartbreaking, troublemaking seductress that she is. I'm telling you, this gal is dangerous! That's why this week we're going to shine the light of God's Word directly on her and expose her for who she really is.

But there's another reason we need to take a long, hard, scriptural look at the Immoral Woman: **we must make sure that our lives bear no resemblance whatsoever to hers.**

2. Read Proverbs 2:16–19, then answer the following questions:

> ¹⁶ *Wisdom will save you from the immoral woman,*
> *from the seductive words of the promiscuous woman.*
> ¹⁷ *She has abandoned her husband*
> *and ignores the covenant she made before God.*
> ¹⁸ *Entering her house leads to death;*
> *it is the road to the grave.*
> ¹⁹ *The man who visits her is doomed.*
> *He will never reach the paths of life.*
>
> —Proverbs 2:16–19

a. In the first line of verse 16, this woman is called "the immoral woman." What is she called in the second line of verse 16, and what does this mean? If you're uncertain, please look for the definition in a dictionary or online at <u>Dictionary.com</u>.

> She's called "the promiscuous woman" which means that she is sexually active and has had a number of sexual partners. In today's culture, it also describes someone who practices "casual sex" or "hooking-up."

b. How does she speak (v. 16)?

> - She speaks seductively.
> - Her words seduce, entice, and tempt.

c.   How does she treat God and others (v. 17)?

> Her commitments to others are meaningless. She abandons even the most intimate relationship – her husband and her marriage – and she ignores her commitment to God.

d.   How dangerous is she?

> She is extremely dangerous. Those who become involved with her will eventually find themselves "doomed" and on "the road to the grave" because she will prevent them from reaching God's path for their lives.

3.   Another description of the Immoral Woman is found in Proverbs 5:3–6. As you read it, circle the words and phrases that are similar to the Proverbs 2:16–19 description

> ³ The **lips** of an immoral woman are as **sweet as honey**,
>   and **her mouth is smoother than oil**.
> ⁴ but the result is bitter as poison,
>   sharp as a double-edged sword.
> ⁵ Her feet go down to **death**;
>   her steps lead straight to the **grave**.
> ⁶ **She does not care about the path to life**.
>   She staggers down a crooked trail and
>   doesn't even realize where it leads.
>
> —Proverbs 5:3–6

4.   Proverbs 30:20 reveals, perhaps, the most dangerous aspect of the Immoral Woman's attitude and character. Part of this verse (from the *NLT*) is recorded for you. Use your Bible to record the shocking final words of this verse (an actual quote from the Immoral Woman herself) in the blank provided.

NOTE: If your Bible translation is hard for you to understand, go online to www.biblegateway.com and read Proverbs 30:20 from another Bible translation such as the New Living Translation, New International Version, or the New American Standard.

> *An adulterous woman consumes a man, then wipes her mouth and says,*
> "   what's wrong with that?   "
>
> —Proverbs 30:20

5. I want you to really think about the quote you just read spoken straight from the lips of the Immoral Woman. Examine her words in Proverbs 30:20, and discover why she's so dangerous by answering the following questions:

    a. What do the Immoral Woman's words reveal about her character and her sense of right and wrong?

    > • She has no sense of right and wrong.
    > • She has low to no moral standards.

    b. What do the Immoral Woman's words reveal about her concern for the guys she seduces and others who may be hurt by her actions?

    > She doesn't care about the guys she hurts nor does she care about the fallout and collateral damage upon others.

    c. As you consider your answers to the previous two questions, why is the Immoral Woman so dangerous to others?

    > She's dangerous because she will do whatever she needs to do to get whatever she wants including destroying the lives of others. And she will do it without remorse or regard for anyone.

6. What insights has the Holy Spirit given you through your study today? How can you use what you've learned?

reflect

> Personal application; answers will vary.

Day Two

pray
$\Big\{$

1. As you begin today's study in prayer, acknowledge your need for wisdom before God. Tell Him that you recognize He is your source for wisdom, and ask Him to speak to you through the pages of His Word.

   For the Lord grants wisdom!
   From his mouth come knowledge and understanding.
   —Proverbs 2:6

Lights, camera, action! The passage you're about to read is written so vividly that it's almost like watching a movie. It is the longest, most descriptive passage ever written about the Immoral Woman in the Scriptures, and it sheds more light on her ways and wiles than any of the passages you studied yesterday. Get ready for an Academy Award-winning performance by a woman playing her part to perfection, our Beauty Don't #1, the **Immoral Woman**.

2. Your primary assignment today is to read and examine Proverbs 7:4–27 and to:

   • Circle any words or phrases used to describe the Immoral Woman's negative character qualities, speech, behavior, and heart.

   • Make notes of your own observations about her and the way she operates in the margins beside this passage.

   To help you get started, I've already circled a couple of words, and you'll also see one of my notes in the margin. I encourage you to fill up the margins with your insights and personal "takes" on the Immoral Woman. The margins of my own copy of this passage are full of notes I've taken and I have to tell you, there's something very empowering about exposing this gal for who she really is.

Proverbs 7:4-27

⁴ *Love wisdom like a sister; make insight a beloved member of your family.*

⁵ *Let them hold you back from an affair with an immoral woman, from listening to the (flattery) of an adulterous woman.*

⁶ *I was looking out the window of my house one day*

⁷ *and saw a simpleminded young man who lacked common sense.*

⁸ *He was crossing the street near the house of an immoral woman. He was strolling down the path by her house*

⁹ *at twilight, as the day was fading, as the dark of night set in.*

She makes the first move; she's one aggressive chick.

¹⁰ *The woman approached him, (dressed seductively) and sly of heart.*

¹¹ *She was the brash, rebellious type who never stays at home.*

¹² *She is often seen in the streets and markets, soliciting at every corner.*

¹³ *She threw her arms around him and kissed him, and with a brazen look she said,*

¹⁴ *"I've offered my sacrifices and just finished my vows.*

¹⁵ *It's you I was looking for! I came out to find you, and here you are!*

¹⁶ *My bed is spread with colored sheets of finest linen imported from Egypt.*

¹⁷ *I've perfumed my bed with myrrh, aloes, and cinnamon.*

¹⁸ *Come, let's drink our fill of love until morning. Let's enjoy each other's caresses,*

¹⁹ *for my husband is not home. He's away on a long trip.*

²⁰ *He has taken a wallet full of money with him, and he won't return until later in the month."*

²¹ *So she seduced him with her pretty speech. With her flattery she enticed him.*

²² *He followed her at once, like an ox going to the slaughter or like a trapped stag,*

²³ *awaiting the arrow that would pierce its heart. He was like a bird flying into a snare, little knowing it would cost him his life.*

²⁴ *Listen to me, my sons, and pay attention to my words.*

²⁵ *Don't let your hearts stray away toward her. Don't wander down her wayward path.*

²⁶ *For she has been the ruin of many; numerous men have been her victims.*

²⁷ *Her house is the road to the grave. Her bedroom is the den of death.*

- vs. 5, 21 she's a flatterer and a flirt
- vs. 10, 13, 15, 18 she's bold, aggressive, and she recognizes an "easy mark" – the type of guy who will fall for her
- v. 10 she dresses seductively
- v. 10 she is sly; she has a hidden agenda
- vs. 11-12 she is brash/loud, rebellious, and she loves to be out and about; she's everywhere in today's culture
- vs. 16-17 she practices pre-meditated promiscuity
- vs. 18-20 she is unfaithful to her husband

Proverbs 7:10 tells us that the Immoral Woman dresses "seductively" which means she dresses with the intent to entice her prey. Her body is her bait, and she makes sure her clothes leave very little to a guy's imagination.

Many teens today are dressing just like the Immoral Woman…and sadly, some of them are Christians. Nancy Leigh DeMoss, a Christian author and teacher (www.reviveourhearts.com), has a wonderful message entitled *Does God Really Care What I Wear?* I love the question in that title. Let's find the answer together right now.

3. Read 1 Timothy 2:9–10 and 1 Peter 3:3–4 and record what you learn about God's dress code for women.

> 1 Timothy 2:9-10 *(NLT)*
> [9] "And I want women to be modest in their appearance. They should wear decent and appropriate clothing and not draw attention to themselves by the way they fix their hair or by wearing gold or pearls or expensive clothes. [10] For women who claim to be devoted to God should make themselves attractive by the good things they do."
>
> 1 Peter 3:3-4 *(NLT)*
> [3] "Don't be concerned about the outward beauty of fancy hairstyles, expensive jewelry, or beautiful clothes. [4] You should clothe yourselves instead with the beauty that comes from within, the unfading beauty of a gentle and quiet spirit, which is so precious to God."

4. Based upon what you've learned today from Proverbs, 1 Timothy, and 1 Peter:

    a. Should the speech, dress, attitude or lifestyle of a Christian woman resemble the Immoral Woman's in any way?

    Yes   **No**

    b. Does God care what we wear?

    Yes   No

    c. Do you think it's possible to dress in a stylish, fashionable way and remain within God's dress code?

    Yes   No

Flirting, flattering, and flaunting it. That's how the Immoral Woman attracts guys. So, maybe you're wondering, "How can a biblically beautiful girl attract a guy?" Well, hang on until we get to Week 5, because in that lesson you're not only going to learn how to attract a guy, you're going to learn how to attract a great guy. But for now, I want you to get the inside scoop about what Christian guys think about modesty and the way girls dress and behave.

5. Alex and Brett Harris (a couple of young, Christian brothers) write a great blog that has blossomed into a movement called "The Rebelution," a "teenage rebellion against low expectations." In response to readers of their blog and discussions on their forums, a modesty survey was conducted to help girls understand how their dress affects guys. The girls submitted questions, the guys responded, and the survey results have been posted online. So here's your assignment:

- Go online right now to www.therebelution.com/modestysurvey/browse.

- In the "select a category" box, click several of the links to see the results of how what you wear and how you behave affects guys. Spend a few minutes browsing the survey results.

- Considering what you've just learned from the Modesty Survey, please answer the following questions:

a. According to the survey, how does the way a girl dresses affect a guy?

> Answers will vary but may include:
> - Guys do notice whether a girl dresses modestly or immodestly.
> - The majority of guys in the survey said that they had less respect for an immodest girl than for a modest one.
> - Many guys also said that modesty is an attractive quality in girls.

b. What are the three most practical things you learned from the survey that will help you dress more modestly?

> Answers will vary but may include:
> - The vast majority of guys believe that modesty is an important quality for their future wife to possess.
> - Because guys struggle with lustful thoughts, they feel "safe" and enjoy being around girls who are modest.
> - Guys don't just recognize immodest clothing; they also notice immodest behavior.

c. According to the survey, modesty isn't just about what you wear. What are some of the other ways you can display modesty especially when you're around guys?

> Answers will vary but may include:
> - Through your behavior
> - Through your words and the topics of your conversation
> - Through physical touch
> - Through the way you make eye contact and look at guys

6. What insights has the Lord revealed to you today, and what does He want you to do with them?

reflect

> Personal application; answers will vary.
>
> _____
>
> _____
>
> _____

NOTE: Another excellent online source that addresses the subject of modesty and Christian dress is an article entitled *Modesty Heart Check*. It includes some fantastic guidelines to help you make godly decisions about how to dress. You really need to check it out. You can find the link to this article at www.girltalk.blogs.com in the April 18, 2006 blog entry. Many of the April 2006 entries deal with the subject of modesty and fashion as well, and I highly recommend that you read and share them with others. The *GirlTalk* blog is one of my favorites.

Day Three

pray

1. As you can see by today's Proverb, the old "ignorance is bliss" philosophy is a lie. In fact, Jesus said, "You shall know the truth, and the truth shall make you free" (John 8:32 *NASB*). Spend a few moments in prayer thanking God for the wisdom, knowledge, and truth He's given you through His liberating, life-changing Word.

> *Wisdom will enter your heart,*
> *and knowledge will fill you with joy.*
> —Proverbs 2:10

Yesterday, you read a very descriptive passage about the Immoral Woman (Proverbs 7). When I studied that passage, I saw something that stunned me. It was in verse 14 where the Immoral Woman says, "I've offered my sacrifices and just finished my vows." I'd seen that verse before but, until then, I'd never noticed the dark reality it reveals: the Immoral Woman is a religious, churchgoing woman.

Don't get me wrong. I'm not saying the Immoral Woman in Proverbs 7 is a Christian. I don't believe she is. But here's what I do know: she does attend church, and she is religious. And based upon Proverbs 7:15 (where she says, "It's you I was looking for!"), I believe she goes to church to hunt for her next victim.

How does all of this apply to you? First of all, you need to be cautious in your relationships (even in your church relationships) because the Immoral Woman has the ability to deceive guys and girls alike. She may even want to be your best friend, so beware.

Secondly, examine your own heart and habits. Are you consciously or unconsciously imitating the Immoral Woman's behavior in your interactions and relationships with guys—even, perhaps, with guys in your church? Girl, don't even go there.

You've seen how the Immoral Woman dresses, speaks, and behaves, but how did she get this way? Where did it all begin? The answers to these questions are critical because they can prevent you from following in her footsteps. So let's get answers from the best and most reliable source of all time: Jesus.

2. Read Mark 7:21–23, and answer the following questions:

   a. According to Jesus, where does immorality (and every other sin) begin?

   > *(NLT)* [21] "For from within, out of a person's heart, come evil thoughts, sexual immorality, theft, murder, [22] adultery, greed, wickedness, deceit, lustful desires, envy, slander, pride, and foolishness. [23] All these vile things come from within; they are what defile you."
   >
   > Immorality begins with our heart.

   b. Your answer to the previous question reveals how the Immoral Woman became an immoral woman. So, how can you keep from following in her footsteps?

   > • By guarding your hearts from immoral and lustful thoughts.
   > • By keeping your hearts pure and clean (1 John 1:9)
   > • By letting Jesus rule and control your hearts and lives.

In the passage you just read, Jesus used the term "sexual immorality" (your Bible may say "adulteries" or "fornications"). You need to know exactly what this means. As an unmarried teen, sexual immorality means any form of pre-marital sexual behavior. And if you get married someday, sexual immorality also means any form of sexual behavior with anyone other than your husband. Therefore, according to Jesus, sex in any form is prohibited unless you are married, and if you're married, sex may only be practiced with your spouse.

You've seen where immorality begins, now discover even more about what Jesus says about sex.

3. Read Matthew 5:27–28, and answer the following questions:

   a. How did Jesus broaden the definition of immorality/adultery in verse 28?

   > *(NLT)* ²⁷ "You have heard the commandment that says, 'You must not commit adultery.' ²⁸ But I say, anyone who even looks at a woman with lust has already committed adultery with her in his heart."
   >
   > Jesus says that immorality also includes immoral thoughts.

   b. In this passage, Jesus is speaking to guys, but would His message also apply to girls? Circle your answer.

   <u>Yes</u>   No

   c. So, when you see a good-looking guy (or when you're even thinking about a guy) what should you be careful NOT to do and why?

   > Girls must be careful not to even fantasize about being with a guy sexually because, according to Jesus, immoral thoughts not only defile us, they can also lead to immoral behavior.

4. What about when a guy looks and lusts after a girl who dresses immodestly or flirts overtly? Is he the only one guilty of immorality? Once again, let's find answers to these questions from Jesus. Read Matthew 18:7, and answer those questions in the space below.

   > *What sorrow awaits the world, because it tempts people to sin.*
   > *Temptations are inevitable, but what sorrow awaits the person*
   > *who does the tempting.* —Matthew 18:7

   > Jesus says that when we tempt others to sin, we are sinning, too. We also will bear the consequences of our sin.

5. In today's culture, sexual temptation is everywhere. Temptation itself is not a sin, but giving in to the temptation (or being the actual tempter) is. Listed below are several very common ways we experience sexual temptation. Complete each sentence by describing a practical way you can resist the temptation and flee from sexual immorality.

- Immoral thoughts and fantasies: I can flee this temptation by _____
  Personal application; answers will vary.

- Immoral television programs: I can flee this temptation by _____
  Personal application; answers will vary.

- Immoral internet sites and ads: I can flee this temptation by _____
  Personal application; answers will vary.

- Immoral reading material (magazines and books): I can flee this temptation by
  Personal application; answers will vary.

- Immoral movies: I can flee this temptation by _____
  Personal application; answers will vary.

- Guys who are flirtatious and/or sexually suggestive in their behavior: I can flee this temptation by _____
  Personal application; answers will vary.

- Girls whose conversation or behavior is sexually suggestive or explicit: I can flee this temptation by _____
  Personal application; answers will vary.

I want to recommend a great resource to you. Covenant Eyes (www.covenanteyes.com) is an internet integrity and accountability program. It monitors every website your computer visits and sends periodic emailed reports of each site visited to an accountability partner of your choice. It's a great way to help you, your family members, or friends to "flee immorality." Check it out!

6. As a result of today's study, what has the Lord revealed to you about the importance of keeping your heart and mind pure?

reflect

> Personal application; answers will vary.

Day Four

pray

1. God is so proud of you! You're taking time today to give Him and His Word priority, and it will make such a difference in your life. I trust you're already seeing the blessings of seeking Him first. Spend a few moments in prayer, thanking Him for enriching your life with His love, wisdom, and guidance.

> *(Wisdom) offers you life in her right hand,*
> *and riches and honor in her left.*
> *She will guide you down delightful paths;*
> *all her ways are satisfying.*
> —Proverbs 3:16–17

In today's world, immorality is the new normality. Retailers, advertisers, TV shows, and the music industry target you with messages that encourage, emphasize, and expect you to be sexually active. And despite the fact that sexually transmitted diseases and teen pregnancy rates are soaring, many people continue to preach the "safe sex" message.

But, precious girl, your heavenly Father wants so much more for you than the world does. As a Father, He wants to protect you and provide the best plan possible for your life. That's why He's given you His Word. He wants to tell you how to live in a way that will please Him and bless you and your future. Listen to Him today, and never forget: He loves you to pieces!

2. Why is sexual purity so important to God? Discover why by reading 1 Corinthians 6:12–20.

1 Corinthians 6:12–20

¹² You say, "I am allowed to do anything"—but not everything is good for you. And even though "I am allowed to do anything," I must not become a slave to anything.

¹³ You say, "Food was made for the stomach, and the stomach for food." (This is true, though someday God will do away with both of them.) But you can't say that our bodies were made for sexual immorality. They were made for the Lord, and the Lord cares about our bodies.

¹⁴ And God will raise us from the dead by his power, just as he raised our Lord from the dead.

¹⁵ Don't you realize that your bodies are actually parts of Christ? Should a man take his body, which is part of Christ, and join it to a prostitute? Never!

¹⁶ And don't you realize that if a man joins himself to a prostitute, he becomes one body with her? For the Scriptures say, "The two are united into one."

¹⁷ But the person who is joined to the Lord is one spirit with him.

¹⁸ Run from sexual sin! No other sin so clearly affects the body as this one does. For sexual immorality is a sin against your own body.

¹⁹ Don't you realize that your body is the temple of the Holy Spirit, who lives in you and was given to you by God? You do not belong to yourself,

²⁰ for God bought you with a high price. So you must honor God with your body.

3. Using 1 Corinthians 6:12–20, answer the following questions:

   a. What did you learn about your body in verse 13?

   > • Our bodies were not made for sexual immorality.
   > • Our bodies were made for the Lord, and He cares about them.

   b. What did you learn about your body and sexual immorality from verses 15–18?

   > • Our bodies are part of Christ.
   > • When we commit sexual sin, we sin against Him.

   c. What clear instruction is given regarding sexual immorality in verse 18?

   > Run – flee, from sexual sin!

d. Why is sexual immorality more serious and detrimental than other kinds of sin (verses 13–18)?

> • Because our bodies belong to God, and He didn't design them for sexual immorality.
> • Because no other sin affects the body like sexual sin does – it is a sin against our own bodies.

e. Who owns the rights to your body, and what is your responsibility regarding your body (verses 19–20)?

> • Our body is the temple of the Holy Spirit.
> • We don't belong to ourselves.
> • God purchased us with the blood of Jesus.
> • We are responsible to honor God with our bodies.

4. The standard for Christian sexuality is stated very simply in 1 Thessalonians 4:3-7. Please read this passage, and answer the questions that follow:

> ³ *God's will is for you to be holy, so stay away from all sexual sin.*
> ⁴ *Then each of you will control his own body and live in holiness and honor—*
> ⁵ *not in lustful passion like the pagans who do not know God and his ways.*
> ⁶ *Never harm or cheat a Christian brother in this matter by violating his wife, for the Lord avenges all such sins, as we have solemnly warned you before.*
> ⁷ *God has called us to live holy lives, not impure lives.*
> —1 Thessalonians 4:3–7

a. What is God's will and sexual standard for you (verses 3a and 7)?

> To be holy; to live a holy life.

b. What does God instruct you to control and how (verses 3b-4)?

> We are commanded to "control our own bodies" by staying "away from all sexual sin."

c. What are the consequences of sexual immorality (verse 6)?

> The Lord will avenge/punish all who are sexually immoral.

5. I cannot close today's study without directing you to one more very important scripture. Pick up your Bible and turn to Hebrews 13:4. Please write that verse (and the warning it contains) in the space below.

> *(NLT)* "Give honor to marriage, and remain faithful to one another in marriage. God will surely judge people who are immoral and those who commit adultery."

6. Respond to everything your heavenly Father has taught you today by writing Him a brief note.

reflect

Dear Father, Personal application; answers will vary.

_____

_____

_____

Day Five

pray

1. Reach out to God today through prayer, embracing Him and the wisdom He's given you this week.

*Wisdom is a tree of life
to those who embrace her;
happy are those who hold her tightly.*
—Proverbs 3:18

Is there hope for an Immoral Woman? Can God forgive an Immoral Woman? Yes and yes! God can and will forgive immorality. But what's more, He can still use us in spite of our past sin…and aren't you glad? Me, too!

If you're struggling with past sin and immorality, may today's study encourage your heart, renew your hope, and reignite your joy.

2. Matthew 1 records the genealogy of Jesus. Read Matthew 1:3–6, then record the female name(s) (mothers) mentioned in the blanks below.

Matthew 1:3–6

³ *Judah was the father of Perez and Zerah (whose mother was Tamar). Perez was the father of Hezron. Hezron was the father of Ram.*

⁴ *Ram was the father of Amminadab. Amminadab was the father of Nahshon. Nahshon was the father of Salmon.*

⁵ *Salmon was the father of Boaz (whose mother was Rahab). Boaz was the father of Obed (whose mother was Ruth). Obed was the father of Jesse.*

⁶ *Jesse was the father of King David. David was the father of Solomon (whose mother was Bathsheba, the widow of Uriah).*

Matthew 1:3 ____Tamar____

Matthew 1:5 ____Rahab____ and ____Ruth____

Matthew 1:6 ____Bathsheba____

Each of these women has something in common: immorality. One disguised herself and seduced her father-in-law (Genesis 38:13–18). Another was a prostitute (Joshua 2:1). One was raised in a city where her family participated in an idolatrous, immoral form of religion (Ruth 1:15). The other committed adultery (2 Samuel 11:2–5).

But immorality isn't the only thing these women have in common. They also shared a common faith in God that led them to repent of their sin and receive His forgiveness. Then God went even one step further. He gave each of them a place in the genealogy of His only begotten Son, Jesus. Why did He do that? I believe He did it to show you and me the "surpassing riches of His grace in kindness toward us in Christ Jesus" (Ephesians 2:7 *NASB*).

All of us need to receive God's forgiveness and grace for our sin, but how can we? The only way possible is by accepting God's gift of salvation through faith in Christ (Ephesians 2:8). You see, Jesus died for our sins, was buried, and rose from the dead to give us salvation, forgiveness from our sins, and eternal life.

Have you ever received God's forgiveness and salvation? God wants you to. Romans 10:9–10 says, "If you confess with your mouth that Jesus is Lord and believe in your heart that God raised him from the dead you will be saved. For it is by believing in your heart that you are made right with God, and it is by confessing with your mouth that you are saved."

If you'd like to receive God's gift of salvation, you can. Right now, tell Him that you want to be forgiven for your sins. Tell Him that you believe Jesus died to save you and rose from the dead to give you eternal life. Invite Him to come into your heart and save you. And when you do that, He will not only save and forgive you, He will also send His Spirit to live within you to enable you to live a life that glorifies and pleases Him (1 Corinthians 6:19–20).

Perhaps you've been a Christian for a while, and maybe you're wondering if God can forgive you of the sins you've committed since you became a Christian. Maybe even the sin of immorality. Absolutely! Truth is, when you were saved God forgave you for ALL of your sins past, present, and future. And here's some awesome news: Your sin cannot affect your salvation or your eternal relationship with God (John 10:28–29).

However, when you sin as a Christian, you grieve and quench the Spirit of God. He responds by convicting you of your sin in order to encourage you to repent and restore fellowship (not relationship – that was settled at salvation) with God. And here's more good news: The Bible says, "If we confess our sins to him, he is faithful and just to forgive us our sins and to cleanse us from all wickedness" (1 John 1:9). If He's convicting you of sin you've never confessed, I encourage you to respond to Him right now. Confess your sin to God and turn away from it. He will forgive and cleanse you, and you will enjoy restored fellowship with Him and a fresh infilling of His Spirit.

3. You've seen the names of several immoral women in the genealogy of Jesus, but pick up your Bible and take a look at Romans 8:15–17. Record what you learn about your own spiritual genealogy. It's beautiful!

> *(NLT)* [15] "So you have not received a spirit that makes you fearful slaves. Instead, you received God's Spirit when he adopted you as his own children. Now we call him, 'Abba, Father.' [16] For his Spirit joins with our spirit to affirm that we are God's children. [17] And since we are his children, we are his heirs. In fact, together with Christ we are heirs of God's glory. But if we are to share his glory, we must also share his suffering."

- At salvation, God adopted us as His children.
- We have every right to call God, "Father."
- Together with Christ, we are heirs of God's glory.

4. I want you to look at one final passage today. Read John 8:3–11, and answer the following questions:

> (NLT) ³ "As he was speaking, the teachers of religious law and the Pharisees brought a woman who had been caught in the act of adultery. They put her in front of the crowd. ⁴ 'Teacher,' they said to Jesus, 'this woman was caught in the act of adultery. ⁵ The law of Moses says to stone her. What do you say?' ⁶ They were trying to trap him into saying something they could use against him, but Jesus stooped down and wrote in the dust with his finger. ⁷ They kept demanding an answer, so he stood up again and said, 'All right, but let the one who has never sinned throw the first stone!' ⁸ Then he stooped down again and wrote in the dust. ⁹ When the accusers heard this, they slipped away one by one, beginning with the oldest, until only Jesus was left in the middle of the crowd with the woman. ¹⁰ Then Jesus stood up again and said to the woman, 'Where are your accusers? Didn't even one of them condemn you?' ¹¹ 'No, Lord,' she said. And Jesus said, 'Neither do I. Go and sin no more.'"

a. How is the woman in this passage described (verse 3)?

> She is described as "a woman who had been caught in the act of adultery."

b. What was Jesus' response and instruction to the woman (verses 10–11)?

> Jesus responded to her in forgiveness and grace, and He instructed her to, "Go and sin no more."

c. What is Jesus teaching us in this passage regarding immorality and any other sin?

> - Jesus forgives all sins – even sexual immorality.
> - Jesus is gracious and loving to sinners, and we are all sinners.
> - We must follow Jesus' example and show love, grace, and forgiveness to those who sin – including ourselves.

5. As you conclude this second week of study, take a few minutes to journal what the Lord has done in your heart by completing the following sentence:

reflect

This week the Lord… | Personal application; answers will vary. |

_____

_____

_____

_____

_____

_____

_____

_____

I learned how to study the Bible from a former Immoral Woman. Kay Arthur—Bible teacher, author, and cofounder of Precept Ministries—is that woman. And I am only one of the thousands upon thousands of lives God has enabled Kay to reach and teach.

Many years ago, when she was a young wife and mother, Kay's husband committed suicide. Soon after that, she spiraled into an immoral lifestyle. She was desperately searching for love, but all she found was sorrow—until she met Jesus. After that, everything about her changed. She hungered for God and began devouring His Word. She became a godly woman—a biblically beautiful woman—and eventually, God led Kay to her husband, Jack Arthur.

Several years after they married, Kay and Jack founded Precept Ministries, and God has blessed, multiplied and grown it into a worldwide outreach. All over the globe, people have learned how to study God's Word through the Bible studies Kay has written and through the excellent training Precept provides.

My dear sister, don't let your past define your present or prevent you from God's plan for your future. Accept His grace and forgiveness through the blood of His Son. Become the biblically beautiful woman He wants you to be. I am so grateful Kay Arthur did.

Week Two • *The Immoral Woman vs. The Godly Woman*

Biblical Beauty Don't: <u>The Immoral Woman:</u>

1) *How does she speak?* Prov. 2:16, 5:3, 7:5, 15, 21
   <u>*Seductive*</u>, flirtatious, flattering, and enticing.

2) *How does she act?* Prov. 7:10–16
   <u>*Aggressive*</u>, brash, rebellious.

3) *How does she dress?* Prov. 7:10
   Seductively, <u>*immodestly*</u>, inappropriately.

4) *What is her heart like?* Prov. 5:6, 30:20, 7:14
   Religious but <u>*ignores*</u> God's ways;
   she <u>*uses*</u> and destroys others with no remorse.

5) *What is her destiny?* Prov. 5:5, 7:27
   Destruction, death, and <u>*judgment*</u>.

Biblical Beauty Do: <u>The Godly Woman:</u>

1) *How does she speak?* 1 Peter 3:4
   <u>*Gentle*</u>, <u>*quiet*</u>, discreet, and edifying.

2) *How does she act?* 1 Peter 3:2, 1 Thess. 4:3–7
   Avoids sexual <u>*immorality*</u>, controls her body so as not to <u>*defraud*</u>
   others. *Defraud = to take advantage of someone; to cause someone to stumble.*

3) *How does she dress?* 1 Timothy 2:9–10
   <u>*modestly*</u>, decently, and <u>*appropriately*</u>.

4) *What is her heart like?* 1 Thess. 4:1, 7
   Longs to <u>*please*</u> God and lead a holy life.

5) *What is her destiny?* 1 Thess. 5:9–10
   Eternal life, salvation, and the <u>*reward*</u> of God's blessing.

Week 3 · *The Indiscreet Woman*

"Granmuhver." It's my new favorite word. It took Ezra, my grandson, almost two years to be able to say it. "Nana" or "Mimi" would have been much easier for him to master, but I come from a long line of "Grandmothers," so that particular title was dear to me. For months and months, Ezra struggled with the formidable three-syllable word. But his perseverance paid off this week as "Granmuhver" rolled off his tongue to the cheers of the very one he addressed.

I think one of the reasons God gives us grandchildren is to give us a second chance to learn what we somehow failed to learn with our own children. Watching Ezra struggle to learn my name has given me a new understanding of God's patience with me.

When I was a young woman, I spent way too much time beating myself up for my failures and lack of spiritual progress. And at times I thought God was even more put out with me than I was. But as a grandmother, I now see what God likely saw back then. He saw me striving and persevering to grow and mature as a Christian, but He also saw there were many formidable three-syllable disciplines that I couldn't master yet...so He patiently waited as I grew.

God's patience. Our perseverance. These are the principles I want to plant in your heart as we begin this week's lesson on the topic of "discretion"—another formidable three-syllable word. It cannot be attained overnight, but as we persevere and God patiently watches, we can become biblically beautiful women of discretion. Little sister, let's persevere 'til we hear God's cheer.

> *Well done, my good and faithful servant.*
> —Matthew 25:21

Day One

pray

1. As you can see by today's Proverb, Wisdom's friends are Prudence, Knowledge, and Discretion. Pray, asking God to show you how to make them your friends, too.

    > *"I, wisdom, dwell together with prudence;*
    > *I possess knowledge and discretion."*
    > —Proverbs 8:12 *NIV*

Allow me to re-introduce you to our Beauty Don't #2, the **Indiscreet Woman**. Unlike the Immoral Woman who is given so much space in the Proverbs, the Indiscreet Woman is only mentioned once. But that single verse packs a real punch. You read it in Week One, but just in case you've forgotten, here it is:

> *A woman who is beautiful but lacks discretion*
> *is like a gold ring in a pig's snout.*
> —Proverbs 11:22

It's kind of funny at first (can't you just picture a proud pig wearing a pretty gold ring?), but that passage isn't just intended to amuse. This proverbial put down also contains a powerful message about the necessity of discretion.

There may only be one verse dedicated to the Indiscreet Woman, but there are plenty of verses in Proverbs that instruct and exhort us to obtain discretion and prudence. Today you'll discover why you need both.

2. Turn back to Week 1, Day 2, number 2, and reacquaint yourself with the definition of "discretion" by reviewing its synonyms.

   In Proverbs 11:22, the word "discretion" means "taste, judgment, and discernment."[3] It can also mean "mental or spiritual perception or discernment."[4] This means the beautiful woman in Proverbs 11:22 had poor taste, bad judgment, no discernment, and lacked mental or spiritual perception. Add all of those ingredients together and you've got a recipe for a disastrous life! Can you see why discretion is so important?

3. Read Proverbs 3:21–26, and record what you learn about the benefits of discretion and the specific ways it can protect you.

   NOTE: Depending on your Bible translation, the word "discretion" may be translated as wise/wisdom, prudent, discernment, or sensible.

   > The benefits of discretion and the way it protects us are underlined in the passage below:
   >
   > *(NLT)* [21] "My child, don't lose sight of common sense and discernment. Hang on to them, [22] <u>for they will refresh your soul. They are like jewels on a necklace.</u> [23] <u>They keep you safe on your way, and your feet will not stumble.</u> [24] <u>You can go to bed without fear; you will lie down and sleep soundly.</u> [25] <u>You need not be afraid of sudden disaster or the destruction that comes upon the wicked,</u> [26] <u>for the LORD is your security. He will keep your foot from being caught in a trap.</u>"

4. What does discretion look like? How does a young woman of discretion behave? And most importantly, how can you know whether or not you possess discretion? The answers to these questions are found in Proverbs as Solomon contrasts the behavior of the discreet and prudent with the foolish, simple, and naïve.

   Read the following verses from Proverbs noting what you learn about the behavior of the discreet versus the behavior of the fool. Keep in mind that prudence, wisdom, and knowledge are synonyms of discretion. To give you a head start, I've completed the first one for you.

   NOTE: To enhance your understanding, you may want to read each verse from two or three Bible translations. One of the simplest ways to access a variety of translations is by visiting www.biblegateway.com. It will also make completing the chart much easier.

Read:	A discreet/prudent person…	But a fool/simple person…
Prov. 12:16 *(NLT)* "A fool is quick-tempered, but a wise person stays calm when insulted."	*overlooks or remains calm when insulted*	*gets angry fast*
Prov. 13:16 *(NLT)* "Wise people think before they act; fools don't—and even brag about their foolishness."	thinks about things and considers the consequences before doing something	doesn't think at all; lives in the moment; boasts about their own foolish decisions
Prov. 14:15 *(NLT)* "Only simpletons believe everything they're told! The prudent carefully consider their steps."	is careful and cautious about what others tell them and what they themselves do	believes anything anyone tells them
Prov. 15:5 *(NLT)* "Only a fool despises a parent's discipline; whoever learns from correction is wise."	learns from correction and from their own mistakes	does not appreciate nor learn from correction and discipline, even when it comes from those who love them most – their parents
Prov. 22:3 *(NLT)* "A prudent person foresees danger and takes precautions. The simpleton goes blindly on and suffers the consequences." *(ESV)* "The prudent sees danger and hides himself, but the simple go on and suffer for it."	sees when trouble or danger is coming and takes the necessary steps to prevent it	whether they foresee trouble or not, they head right into harm's way and will suffer for it

5. Ask God to show you one or two specific areas in your life where you need to develop discretion and prudence. Record your insights.

reflect

Personal application; answers will vary.

Day Two

pray

1. You have influence. Whether it's with your friends or family, your life influences others. Are you advising them wisely? Are you helping them succeed? Your responsibility as a young woman of influence is huge. Get on your knees right now and ask God to give you wisdom in your relationships, conversations and dealings with others.

"Good advice and success belong to me (wisdom).
Insight and strength are mine.
Because of me, kings reign, and rulers make just laws.
Rulers lead with my help, and nobles make righteous judgments."
—Proverbs 8:14–16

We spent yesterday entirely in Proverbs, but today we are going to get out and meet one of the most fascinating women in the Bible. Her name is Abigail, and she's a role model of discretion, prudence and wisdom. I think you're going to love her. She's certainly taught me a lot—can't wait to meet her one day! Enjoy your time today with Abigail.

2. Pick up your Bible and get to know Abigail by reading 1 Samuel 25:1–42, then record your insights to the following questions:

> NOTE: Because of length of this passage, it is not printed for you here. Please reference it at the back of the Teacher Guide on pages 176-177.

a. What kind of woman was Abigail? How was she described (verse 3)?

> Abigail was sensible (intelligent/wise/prudent) and beautiful.

b.   What was her husband like (verse 3)?

> Her husband, Nabal, was harsh, crude, mean, and evil.

c.   When David's men requested payment for services they had provided to Nabal (they had protected Nabal's shepherds and his sheep), Nabal foolishly refused to pay (verses 4–11). As a result, David and his men planned to kill Nabal and his entire household (verses 12–13, 21–22). But one of Nabal's servants told Abigail about everything that was about to happen and asked her to get involved. What did Abigail do (verses 18–31)?

> Abigail made the decision to send David and his men the payment they deserved, but she didn't tell her husband – both she and her servants knew that no one could talk him out of his foolish decision (v. 17). She also went bravely and quickly to meet David in person.

d.   How did Abigail's actions and speech reveal her discretion, prudence, and wisdom?

> - Her actions and intervention protected the lives of many innocent people and prevented David (who would later become king) from committing murder.
> - Her words to David were both true and respectful.
> - Abigail wisely and tactfully reminded David that what he was about to do was wrong (murder).
> - She also helped David see that God was trying to protect him from committing such an awful sin and suffering untold consequences.
> - She reminded David of God's promises to him.

e.   What immediate benefits did Abigail receive because of her discretion and prudence (verses 34–35)?

> - The gratitude and appreciation of a future king: David.
> - The promise that David would not avenge Nabal and his household.

f. What happened to Nabal (verses 37–38)?

> ³⁷ "In the morning when Nabal was sober, his wife told him what had happened. As a result he had a stroke, and he lay paralyzed on his bed like a stone. ³⁸ About ten days later, the LORD struck him, and he died."

g. What future benefits did Abilgail receive because of her discretion and prudence (verses 39–42)?

> • A proposal of marriage from David, the future king.
> • Abigail became David's wife.

3. We all have to deal with foolish, difficult people at times. What insights did you learn from Abigail to help you deal with the Nabals in your life?

reflect

> Personal application; answers will vary.
>
> _____
>
> _____
>
> _____

Day Three

pray

1. As you read today's Proverb, I hope you are encouraged by God's invitation to freely give you wisdom. Take Him up on His offer. Ask Him to give you wisdom as you study His Word today.

   Listen as Wisdom calls out! Hear as understanding raises her voice!
   … At the entrance to the city, at the city gates, she cries aloud,
   "I call to you, to all of you! I am raising my voice to all people.
   How naïve you are! Let me give you some common sense.
   O foolish ones, let me give you understanding."
   —Proverbs 8:1–5

"Discretion" used to be one of those innocuous, vanilla-sounding words that I associated with…well, "boring." I knew it was closely related to the word "prudent" (another unpopular, seldom-used word) but to be honest, both words were a little yawn inducing to me. Not anymore.

God's Word has completely changed the negative connotations I used to associate with the words "discretion" and "prudence." Although I don't often use those specific words (and I'm guessing you probably don't either), I do use positive terms like "smart," "discerning," "spiritually sharp," and "wise" to describe discreet, prudent people.

Whatever you may choose to call them, discretion and prudence are keys that can unlock your God-given potential. My goal today is to take you into God's Word where He can whet your appetite to live up to that potential. My prayer is that you will take what He teaches you and run with it.

2. Yesterday, when you studied Abigail, you also met David. Today, we'll go back to an earlier period of David's life when he was a young shepherd living at home with his family. Read 1 Samuel 16:14–22 and answer the following questions:

> NOTE: Because of length of this passage, it is not printed for you here. Please reference it at the back of the Teacher Guide on page 178.

a. In this passage, you learned that David was a skillful musician, but what did you learn about his character (verse 18)?

> • David was a brave warrior.
> • David was young, yet he had good judgment (i.e., discretion, prudence).
> • It was obvious to others that the Lord was with David.

b. What was the result of David's discretion and prudence (verses 19–22)?

> • David was sought after by King Saul to serve him.
> • King Saul loved David and promoted him to become Saul's armor bearer.
> • King Saul was so pleased with David that he asked David's father for his permission for David to remain with Saul.

3. Joseph, another Old Testament character, was a young man whose jealous brothers sold him to slave traders who, in turn, took him to Egypt. While he was there, Joseph was wrongly convicted and jailed. But because of his God-given ability to interpret dreams, he was eventually summoned to appear before Pharaoh to interpret Pharaoh's dream. Read Genesis 41:38–44, and answer the following questions:

> NOTE: Because of length of this passage, it is not printed for you here. Please reference it at the back of the Teacher Guide on page 178.

a. What did you learn about Joseph's character in this passage (verses 38–39)?

> • It was obvious to everyone that Joseph was filled with the spirit of God.
> • Joseph was more wise and intelligent than anyone in Pharaoh's kingdom.

b. What was the result of Joseph's discretion, discernment, and wisdom (verses 40–44)?

> • Joseph was promoted from the prison to the palace.
> • Joseph was put in charge of Pharaoh's court; only Pharaoh outranked him.
> • Joseph was put in charge of the entire nation of Egypt.
> • Joseph was given the king's ring symbolizing that he had the king's authority.
> • Joseph was dressed in the finest clothes and jewelry.
> • Joseph was given a chariot symbolizing that he was second-in-command.
> • Everyone, except Pharaoh, had to follow Joseph's command.

4. David and Joseph were both young when they began serving King Saul and Pharaoh. What does this reveal about discretion, wisdom, and discernment? Before you answer this question, read Proverbs 20:11 for additional insight (and keep in mind, this verse applies to both guys and gals).

> *(NLT)* "Even children are known by the way they act, whether their conduct is pure, and whether it is right."
>
> You do not have to be an adult to be wise, discreet, and prudent. Even the young can possess these qualities and, if they do, it will be evident by the way they act and speak. Wisdom is proven through conduct.

5. As a young woman, what insights have you learned today to apply to your own life? How are you doing when it comes to discretion?

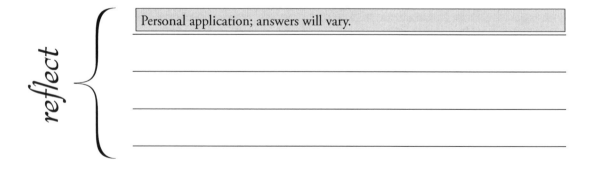

reflect

> Personal application; answers will vary.

Day Four

pray

1. One of the things I love the most about the incredibly prudent group of Old Testament characters we have studied over the past two days is their humility. Humble yourself before the Lord today in prayer, and ask Him to help you stay that way.

   > *Don't be impressed with your own wisdom.*
   > *Instead, fear the Lord and turn away from evil.*
   > —Proverbs 3:7

In your study of Abigail, David, and Joseph, you have seen real-life examples of what discretion looks like. You have also seen the powerful way God can use those who possess it. Today you will meet another incredible Old Testament character: Daniel.

It is my heartfelt prayer that God will use Abigail, David, Joseph, and Daniel to inspire and encourage you to become a modern-day example of discretion before your family and friends. May all who know you witness the biblical beauty mark of discretion upon your life.

2. Daniel was a young Jewish teen who was taken into Babylonian captivity where he served King Nebuchadnezzar. One night, the king had a dream, and none of his magicians or wise men could interpret it. As a result, Nebuchadnezzar ordered their deaths and the deaths of Daniel and his friends. Read the following passages and questions, and record what you learn:

   a. Daniel 2:12–19—What did you learn about Daniel's character (verses 14, 16–19)?

   > NOTE: Because of length of this passage, it is not printed for you here. Please reference it at the back of the Teacher Guide on page 179.
   >
   > - Even in the face of extreme circumstances, Daniel handled himself with wisdom and discretion.
   > - Daniel did not waste time; he went directly to the king to request more time.
   > - Daniel had godly friends, and he enlisted them to pray.
   > - When God revealed the secret to Daniel, he praised God – he was humble.

   b. Daniel 2:46–48—What was the result of Daniel's wisdom, discretion, and prudence?

   > *(NLT)* [46] "Then King Nebuchadnezzar threw himself down before Daniel and worshiped him, and he commanded his people to offer sacrifices and burn sweet incense before him. [47] The king said to Daniel, 'Truly, your God is the greatest of gods, the LORD over kings, a revealer of mysteries, for you have been able to reveal this secret.' [48] Then the king appointed Daniel to a high position and gave him many valuable gifts. He made Daniel ruler over the whole province of Babylon, as well as chief over all his wise men."

3. Joseph, David, Abigail, and Daniel all shared: 1) a common faith in God, and 2) the attributes of discretion, prudence, discernment, and wisdom. But there's something else they shared in common, and here's a hint: what happened to each of them after their discretion and prudence was recognized by others?

> - Each of them were recognized for being wise, prudent, and intelligent by those in authority over them.
> - Each of them were promoted and rewarded for their wisdom, prudence, and intelligence.
> - Those in authority often recognize the characteristics of discretion in others.

Friendships are so important but, sadly, a lack of discretion can destroy even the best of friendships. Girl, let's just call it what it really is: gabbing and gossiping. We've both been guilty of it, and we've both been hurt by it. Our final study today will remind us of the dangers of indiscretion and the blessings of just plain ol' keeping our mouths shut.

4. Read the following scriptures, and record what you learn about the dangers of indiscretion, the blessings of discretion, and how to preserve precious friendships:

   a. Proverbs 11:13

   > *(NLT)* "A gossip goes around telling secrets, but those who are trustworthy can keep a confidence."
   > - Those who gossip are untrustworthy and indiscreet.
   > - But those who don't gossip are trustworthy.

   b. Proverbs 16:28

   > *(NLT)* "A troublemaker plants seeds of strife; gossip separates the best of friends."
   > - Those who "plant seeds of strife" are trouble.
   > - Indiscretion and gossip can tear apart even the best of friends.

   c. Proverbs 17:9

   > *(NLT)* "Love prospers when a fault is forgiven, but dwelling on it separates close friends."
   >
   > *(NASB)* "He who conceals a transgression seeks love, but he who repeats a matter separates intimate friends."
   > - A wise and discreet person will forgive the faults of others without broadcasting those faults to others.
   > - Broadcasting the faults of others can break up close friends.

d. Proverbs 21:23

> *(NLT)* "Watch your tongue and keep your mouth shut, and you will stay out of trouble."
>
> One of the blessings of discretion is that it will keep you out of trouble.

e. Proverbs 26:20

> *(NLT)* "Fire goes out without wood, and quarrels disappear when gossip stops."
>
> •   Gossip and indiscretion cause quarrels and division.
> •   When you hear others gossiping and quarreling, use discretion: don't add fuel to the fire.

5. Have you ever been hurt by gossip? If so, describe the damage it did and the toll it took on you. Also, describe how it affected your relationship with the gossip.

> Personal application; answers will vary.

6. Finally, as you reflect upon your own relationships, how and with whom are you most challenged to be discreet? What specific, scriptural steps can you take to become a woman of discretion and not a gossip?

reflect

> Personal application; answers will vary.
> _____
> _____
> _____
> _____

Day Five

pray

1. Everyone wants to have joy, and those who follow wisdom usually do. Take a few minutes to praise and thank God for the joy He has brought you, and for the sorrow He has saved you from all because of the wisdom He has given you.

> *"My children, listen to me (wisdom),*
> *for all who follow my ways are joyful.*
> *...Joyful are those who listen to me,*
> *watching for me daily at my gates,*
> *waiting for me outside my home."*
> —Proverbs 8:32–34

Discretion and prudence are in short supply in today's world. Are you ready to begin making up for that deficit? You can. God has given you everything you need to become a woman of influence and discretion. And as you have seen in your homework this week, one discreet woman can make a huge difference in so many lives. May your study today encourage you to step up and be that woman.

2. Prudence and discretion are synonymous with wisdom, and one of the most encouraging promises about wisdom is found in James 1:5–8. Find out how to get wisdom by reading this passage and answering the following questions:

> ⁵ *If you need wisdom, ask our generous God, and He will give it to you. He will not rebuke you for asking..*
> ⁶ *But when you ask Him, be sure that your faith is in God alone. Do not waver, for a person with divided loyalty is as unsettled as a wave of the sea that is blown and tossed by the wind.*
> ⁷ *Such people should not expect to receive anything from the Lord.*
> ⁸ *Their loyalty is divided between God and the world, and they are unstable in everything they do.*

a. How can you receive wisdom (verse 5)?

> By asking God for wisdom.

b. Who is the source of wisdom (verse 5)?

> God is the source of wisdom.

c. What are the requirements for receiving wisdom (verse 6a)?

> You must place your faith in God alone.

d. Who should not expect to receive wisdom (verses 6b–8)?

> - Those who are disloyal to God will not receive wisdom.
> - When you go back and forth between God's wisdom and the world's wisdom, you will be unstable in all of your ways.

e. So, what's the first thing you should do the next time you need wisdom?

> Seek God – pray and depend upon His Word – first and foremost.

3. Now let's focus on two other areas in your life that will greatly determine your ability to grow in wisdom and discretion. Read the following verses and record what you learn about how to grow in wisdom:

a. Psalm 119:97–100

> *(NLT)* [97] "Oh, how I love your instructions! I think about them all day long. [98] Your commands make me wiser than my enemies, for they are my constant guide. [99] Yes, I have more insight than my teachers, for I am always thinking of your laws. [100] I am even wiser than my elders, for I have kept your commandments."
> - Seek and meditate upon God's Word
> - Obey God's Word

b.   Proverbs 13:20

> *(NLT)* "Walk with the wise and become wise; associate with fools and get in trouble."
> •   Spend time with wise people and friends.

c.   1 Peter 2:2

> *(NLT)* "Like newborn babies, you must crave pure spiritual milk so that you will grow into a full experience of salvation. Cry out for this nourishment."
> •   Wisdom and spiritual growth are the result of feeding upon God's Word regularly.
> •   Like a baby cries out when it is hungry, we must cry out to God and depend upon Him for spiritual nourishment and wisdom.

Girl, you're on your way to becoming a biblical beauty because guess what? You've just completed the first half of our study. Thank you for your dedication and commitment! I'm so proud of you!

My favorite Old Testament verse says, "And He humbled you and let you be hungry, and fed you with manna which you did not know, nor did your fathers know, that He might make you understand that man does not live by bread alone, but man lives by everything that proceeds out of the mouth of the Lord" (Deuteronomy 8:3 *NASB*). I'm praying you're feeling really full right now because of the feast God has fed you over the past three weeks. God bless you for giving His Word priority!

4.   Spend a few minutes journaling what the Lord has done in your heart this week through His Word by completing the following sentence:

reflect {

This week the Lord… | Personal application; answers will vary. |

_____

_____

_____

_____

_____

I was having a very difficult time with a very difficult person. Nothing I could say or do seemed to improve the relationship, and I could not understand why. It was a puzzle I could not solve. What I needed was a great, big, heaping dose of discretion—but I didn't know that. Thank God, He did. And He knew just the woman who could give it to me.

One evening while I was at a friend's house, I picked up a book she had by an author I had heard of but had never read before. As I perused through its pages, I was astonished; it described my difficult relationship in detail. I borrowed that book, took it straight home, and read it all night. And somewhere in the wee hours of the morning, God used the words of that author to give me the wisdom I needed to deal with that relationship the right way. The prudent way. The discreet way.

Since that time, I have read almost every book Jan Silvious has written. A gifted author, speaker, and Christian counselor, Jan is also an amazing woman of discretion and discernment. I am serious when I tell you that you need to get your hands on every book she has written. Practical, biblical, witty, and intelligent, Jan epitomizes the biblically beautiful attributes of prudence and discretion.

As I've said before, we can't become women of discretion overnight. But spending time with wonderful authors like Jan Silvious can get us there a whole lot faster.

Want to find out more about

Jan Silvious
and her books?

Visit her online at
www.jansilvious.com

Week Three • *The Indiscreet Woman vs. The Woman of Discretion*

OT synonyms for discretion:
discreet, discerning, prudent, understanding, insight, wise

NT synonyms for discretion:
discreet, sensible, sober, self-controlled, wisdom

Biblical Beauty Don't:
The Indiscreet Woman:

1) She *talks* too much and *says* whatever comes into her head.

2) She *yawns* at personal and *spiritual* growth.

3) She makes *poor decisions* based on bad judgment.

4) She's *moody* and enjoys *drama*.

5) She *flirts* with danger and *invites* it.

Biblical Beauty Do:
The Discreet Woman:

1) She *controls* her *tongue* and speaks with wisdom. *Prov. 10:13, 11:12*

2) She's eager to learn, *grow*, and mature *spiritually*. *Prov. 14:6*

3) She makes *wise decisions* based on truth. *Prov. 13:16, 14:15*

4) She is *even-tempered* and not easily angered. *Prov. 17:27*

5) She *recognizes* danger and *avoids* it. *Prov. 27:12*

Week 4 • *The Irritating Woman*

Wouldn't you know it. Mere seconds before I began writing this lesson on the Beauty Don't #3—the **Irritating Woman**—I opened my mouth and became that woman. I should have seen it coming.

Clue #1: My husband Bill had been doing a small home repair project. Home repair projects seldom go smoothly at the Cole house. This should have alerted me to the very real possibility that things could be heading south fast.

Clue #2 came in the form of a question: "Do we have an X-ACTO® knife?" Bill asked. Scary. So, I took a deep breath and replied, "Yes, it's in the pantry in the tool drawer." But I knew I should also have said, "Let me go get it and bring it to you." But I didn't. I didn't want to. "Let him get it," I thought to myself. "He's a big boy." And that sassy little selfish attitude was Clue #3—I should have known what was about to happen.

Less than five minutes later, that contentious, crabby Irritating Woman appeared.

I walked into the room where Bill was doing the repair, and to my absolute horror I discovered he wasn't using an X-ACTO® knife. No, turns out, he couldn't find the X-ACTO® knife so he was using one of my very best kitchen knives. That man was carving into drywall with my good knife! Gasping then erupting, I exploded. Words gushed from my mouth…followed by silence. Too much silence if you know what I mean.

Fortunately, I have a very forgiving husband. After I apologized, peace prevailed. But oh, how I hate it when I foolishly ignore every obvious clue around me and give in to the Irritating Woman.

I wonder. Has the Irritating Woman shown up at your house lately? Have your friends or teachers ever met her? Wouldn't you like to banish bossy ol' Beauty Don't #3 and replace her with her biblically beautiful counterpart the Edifying Woman? Well then, this lesson is for you. Oh, who am I kidding? This lesson is for me, too.

Day One

pray {

1. The message of today's proverb is obvious. Ask God to take the limp out of your spiritual walk by committing to be led by His wisdom.

> *If you live a life guided by wisdom,*
> *you won't limp or stumble as you run.*
> —Proverbs 4:12

The Irritating Woman is mentioned five times in Proverbs, and each time it says practically the same thing. So why would God repeat Himself five times?

I believe it's because He wants to emphasize a message that He doesn't want us girls to miss.

But I think there's another reason why God mentions the Irritating Woman five times. It's because He loves us—and He "gets" us girls, too. Hold on to that thought as we begin our study of the ugly, unlikable woman none of us want to be, Beauty Don't #3.

2. Read each verse about the Irritating Woman, and answer the questions that follow.

   NOTE: The verses below are taken from the *New Living Translation*, but in other Bible translations, the word "woman" is used instead of "wife." Therefore, these verses apply to all women of all ages, not just married women. Also, the word "contentious" means quarrelsome and argumentative.[5]

   A nagging *wife* annoys *like a* constant dripping.
   —Proverbs 19:13

   *It is better to live alone in the corner of an attic
   than with a* contentious *wife in a lovely home.*
   —Proverbs 21:9

   *It is better to live alone in the desert
   than with a* crabby, complaining *wife.*
   —Proverbs 21:19

   *It is better to live alone in the corner of an attic
   than with a* quarrelsome *wife in a lovely home.*
   —Proverbs 25:24

   A quarrelsome *wife is as* annoying *as
   a* constant dripping *on a rainy day.
   Stopping her* complaints *is like trying to stop the wind
   or trying to hold something with greased hands.*
   —Proverbs 27:15–16

   a. How is the Irritating Woman described? Answer this question by circling the specific adjectives used to describe her in the verses above.

   b. Now let's broaden our perspective about the Irritating Woman. What are some synonyms for the words you just circled? What do you call a girl or woman like this (careful!)? Record several synonyms.

   > Many answers are possible but may include:
   > - A nag
   > - A crab
   > - A pain; a pain-in-the-neck
   > - Grumpy; a grouch
   > - Aggravating; infuriating; exasperating; frustrating; irritating
   > - Short-tempered; a woman with a short fuse
   > - Mean; nasty
   > - A witch

c. As you look at the words you circled and the synonyms you found, it's easy to see the downside of having to hang out with an Irritating Woman whether she's young or old. In fact, three of the five verses begin with the same six words, and they describe exactly how she makes other people feel. Record those words in the blanks below.

It	is	better	to	live	alone

d. Think about the six words you just recorded, and answer these questions: If that's how an irritating girl or woman makes people feel, what choice will they eventually make? What will ultimately happen to her?

> People will probably decide to keep their distance, avoid, or stay away from her altogether. As a result, the irritating girl (or woman) will ultimately find herself left out, unpopular, and alone.

3. One example of the dangerous consequences of becoming an Irritating Woman is found in 2 Samuel 6:12-23. It details an encounter between King David and his wife, Michal. Read this passage, picturing it in your mind as you read, and answer the following questions:

> NOTE: Because of length of this passage, it is not printed for you here. Please reference it at the back of the Teacher Guide on page 180. Also, an ephod (v. 14) was a simple robe worn primarily by priests of that day. Therefore, David was not uncovered as Michal sarcastically claimed (v. 20).

a. What did David do that provoked Michal, and what does this reveal about her heart and her own relationship with the Lord (verse 16a)?

> David was celebrating and dancing before the Lord (v. 14) because the Ark of God (the symbol of God's presence) was being brought into the city of David. Michal was not participating in the celebration with her husband and all of the people. This reveals that her heart for the Lord wasn't at all like David's.

b. Before Michal ever said a word to David, what had she already done (verse 16b)?

> She had filled her heart with contempt and disgust for David.

c. Note how the conversation between Michal and David began (verse 20).
Who started it, and what does this tell you?

> Michal went out to confront David. She was angry and disgusted with him. She
> wanted to give him a piece of her mind.

d. How would you describe Michal's words to David?

> Michal's words were sarcastic, bitter, and intentionally hurtful. She wanted to
> shame and hurt David for what he'd done.

e. What consequences did Michal experience in her life and marriage as a result
of her words and attitude (v. 23)?

> Michal never bore any children. This likely means that David never slept with her
> again. Michal's irritating behavior cost her dearly.

I am embarrassed to share this, but I must confess. When I was your age,
I spent way too much time in critical, complaining, Irritating Woman mode. I cut
down and criticized others regularly, and I complained and whined about, well,
almost everything.

When I think about the negativity and tension I caused in my relationships
at home and at school back then, it makes me cringe. And you know what? That
Irritating Woman never did really work for me. In fact, I'm pretty sure she worked
against me. As I recall, my name never came anywhere close to making the ballot
for Class Favorite. But if Class Critic had been up for vote, yikes!

4. So, what about you, my precious, young friend. Has the Irritating Woman
shown up in your life lately? What will you do today to prevent from becoming a
full-fledge, Irritating Woman deluxe (like Michal) in the future?

reflect

> Personal application; answers will vary.
> _____
>
> _____
>
> _____
>
> _____

Day Two

pray

1. The Irritating Woman seems to bring out the worst in others. Her crabbiness and contentiousness pushes everybody's buttons. So what can you do to prevent from being sucked in? To answer that question, read today's proverb. Then pray and ask God to protect you the next time an Irritating Woman starts to get on your last nerve.

> *Wisdom will save you from evil people,*
> *from those whose speech is corrupt.*
> —Proverbs 2:12

Yesterday, you saw the dangers and consequences of becoming an Irritating Woman. She annoys and aggravates others, she offends her friends, and she can even undermine and destroy her own marriage. Anyone can see the fallout of her flawed behavior—a path of destruction follows her everywhere she goes. And if she refuses to change, her life will devolve into a series of broken relationships.

If the downside of becoming an Irritating Woman is so obvious, then why do we girls struggle so hard with giving in and becoming just like her? Let's get to the root of our universal problem in today's study.

2. Where did the Irritating Woman come from? Uncovering and understanding her past (and ours) will empower us from being overpowered by her. Genesis 3 records the fall of man—the sin of Adam and Eve—and the resulting consequences. Read God's words to Eve from the translations provided, and answer the questions that follow:

> *To the woman He said, "I will greatly multiply Your pain in childbirth,*
> *In pain you will bring forth children; Yet your desire will be for your husband,*
> *And he will rule over you."*
> —Genesis 3:16 (*NASB*)

> *Then he said to the woman, "I will sharpen the pain of your pregnancy,*
> *and in pain you will give birth. And you will desire to control your husband,*
> *but he will rule over you."*
> —Genesis 3:16

a. How did the fall (sin) change the dynamics of Eve's relationship with Adam?

> • After the fall, Eve desired to control Adam.
> • Designed by God to be Adam's helper (Gen. 2:18), Eve will now struggle in that role.

b. Who has God called to be the leader of the home, and why is that such a challenge for women?

> From the beginning, God created the man to the leader of the home. This was not a problem for the woman in the beginning. But now, because of sin and the results of the fall, allowing the husband to lead *is* a challenge because wives desire to control (lead) their husbands.

Genesis reveals the root problem of the Irritating Woman: sin and a desire to control others. It also opens the door to another topic that is a sore subject with some women: submission. Now I realize that marriage may be a long way off for you, but you're probably already thinking about Mr. Right and hoping to marry someday. But, precious girl, before you ever even meet him, you really need to know what the Bible teaches about submission. Why? Because it will help you choose the right Mr. Right!

The Bible teaches clearly that wives are to submit to their own husbands (not to every man, but to their own husbands). It also teaches that husbands are to love their wives as Christ loved the church (Ephesians 5:22–33). **Submission basically means that women are to respectfully place themselves under the authority of their husbands.** That's why it's so important that you choose the right kind of man to marry (which will be the focus of next week's lesson), a man whose authority you respect.

The scriptural principles of submission, however, *do not imply that women are inferior to men.* On the contrary, Scripture emphasizes the equality of men and women: "God created man in His own image, in the image of God He created Him; male and female He created them" (Genesis 1:27 *NASB*). But even before the fall of man, Adam and Eve had different roles. From the beginning, God created man to lead the home and woman to be his helper (Genesis 2:18). Eve's submission to Adam wasn't a problem before they sinned, but it became a major problem after they sinned.

Now just in case you're upset (or a little offended) by the concept of submission, please take time to read Philippians 2:5–11. This beautiful passage reveals that Christ—who is equal with God—willingly submitted Himself to God when He came to this earth and died on the cross to save us. In this way, Christ is an example to everyone (men and women alike) of the beauty and importance of submission.

One final point on this topic: submission is not unconditional. A wife is not required to submit to abuse or to ongoing sexual infidelity and immorality. When abuse occurs, a wife should seek protection from civil authorities as well as support from her church. When there is infidelity or immorality, a wife should seek sound, biblical Christian counsel.

Are married women the only ones who struggle with the desire to control others and the contentious, complaining attitude that desire breeds? No. Every woman young or old, single or married—every descendant of Eve— struggles with it, even spiritually mature women, and you're about to meet one of them.

3. Miriam was the older sister of Moses and Aaron. All three siblings were leaders over the Israelites, but God gave Moses authority over Miriam and Aaron (even though Moses was the youngest). God also chose Moses to be His #1 spokesman. A chilling encounter between Miriam, Aaron, and Moses is recorded in Numbers 12:1–15. Use your Bible to read this passage, and then answer the following questions:

> NOTE: Because of length of this passage, it is not printed for you here. Please reference it at the back of the Teacher Guide on page 181. Also, the Cushites were not Israelites, but Israelites were not prohibited by God from marrying Cushites.

a. What caused Miriam to become an Irritating Woman (v. 1-2)? In other words, what set her off?

> • Miriam was upset that her brother, Moses, had married a Cushite woman.
> • Miriam also was upset because she felt that she was as much a spokesperson for God as Moses was.

b. What do Miriam's words reveal about her heart? Do you think jealousy could have been the root of her contentious, complaining behavior?

> Answers will vary, but may include:
> • Words do reveal the heart (Mark 7:21-23), and Miriam's critical words came from a critical heart.
> • Jealousy was very likely the root cause of Miriam's complaints and criticism.
> • She may have been jealous of Moses' new wife or upset that he had made a choice that she couldn't control.
> • She also may have been jealous because Moses' (her younger brother) was also in a position of leadership over her.

c. What do you think Miriam sought to gain by her quarrelsome complaints? In other words, what payoff do you think she was seeking?

> Answers will vary, but may include:
> • Miriam's criticism was her effort to tear him down and make herself look better.

d. What was Miriam's actual payoff (vs. 4–15)?

> Miriam's actual payoff was God's judgment, leprosy, and being disciplined publicly and shamed.

4. You've seen what set Miriam off, but think about yourself for a minute. Record one or two things that have set off the Irritating Woman in you lately.

> Personal application; answers will vary.

5. Who are the primary earthly authority figures in your life (for example: your parents, teachers, church leaders, etc.). Write their names in the following blanks, and circle the phrase that best describes your current level of respect and attitude toward them.

    > Personal application; answers will vary.

	very respectful	mostly respectful	respect varies frequently	mostly disrespectful	very disrespectful
_____	very respectful	mostly respectful	respect varies frequently	mostly disrespectful	very disrespectful
_____	very respectful	mostly respectful	respect varies frequently	mostly disrespectful	very disrespectful
_____	very respectful	mostly respectful	respect varies frequently	mostly disrespectful	very disrespectful
_____	very respectful	mostly respectful	respect varies frequently	mostly disrespectful	very disrespectful
_____	very respectful	mostly respectful	respect varies frequently	mostly disrespectful	very disrespectful
_____	very respectful	mostly respectful	respect varies frequently	mostly disrespectful	very disrespectful

6. It's time to dethrone that cranky, critical, complaining Irritating Woman who wants to run (and possibly ruin) your life. If you've been an Irritating Woman lately, write a brief sentence confessing your sin to the Lord, and receive His forgiveness. Then take the next step: Ask anyone who has witnessed and/or been the object of your Irritating Woman behavior to forgive you.

reflect

> Personal application; answers will vary.

_____

_____

_____

Day Three

pray

1. Wisdom wants to be your sister and best friend—and you could have none better. Ask God to help you get to know Wisdom well so that your friendship with her will flourish and bear much fruit.

> *Say to wisdom, "You are my sister,"*
> *and call insight your intimate friend.*
> —Proverbs 7:4 *RSV*

I don't know about you, but I'm worn out from spending the past two days with irritating women. First there was Michal who taught us how to lose a good man. Then there was Miriam who taught us how to rile God's anger through jealousy, envy, and a critical, complaining spirit.

So today, let's hang out with some cool-headed chicks you've probably never met before: Mahlah, Noah, Hoglah, Milcah and Tirzah, also known as "the daughters of Zelophehad." These gals really know how to handle themselves, and the beautiful thing about them is this: they know how to get what they want without crabbing, complaining, or controlling. By the time you've finished reading about them, you may even want to name one of your future daughters after them—probably not "Hoglah" though!

Enjoy your time with the five biblically beautiful daughters of Zelophehad.

2. Your assignment is simple. Read the following passages, and record your answers to the questions on the chart.

> NOTE: Because of length of these two passages, they are not printed for you here. Please reference them at the back of the Teacher Guide on pages 182-183.

- Numbers 27:1–11: This passage tells about a meeting the sisters had with Moses. Their meeting occurred after a census had been taken to determine the adult male population of each tribe of Israel. Results from the census would enable Moses to determine how much land each tribe would receive. At that time, only males could inherit land.

- Numbers 36:1–12: This passage tells about another meeting Moses had with the male relatives of the daughters of Zelophehad.

The Daughters of Zelophehad	
What problems and complications did they face (Num. 27:3–4, 36:1–4)?	How did they handle their problems, and what characteristics did they display?
<ul><li>Their father had died without sons/heirs.</li><li>This meant that his name would "disappear."</li><li>It also meant that his descendants (his daughters) would not be recognized or given property in his name.</li></ul>	<ul><li>They presented a petition/request to Moses and Israel's leaders.</li><li>They presented it themselves in person which required strength and courage.</li><li>They sought change and justice in a reasonable, respectful way.</li></ul>

How would an Irritating Woman handle problems like these?	How would others ultimately benefit from the way they handled their problem (Num. 27:8–11)?
<ul><li>By getting angry and complaining and criticizing endlessly.</li><li>By stirring up trouble and seeking to undermine the authority of those in leadership.</li><li>By nagging and manipulating others to try to get what they want.</li><li>By arguing their case instead of presenting in in a reasonable, respectful way.</li></ul>	<ul><li>Fathers who died without sons could now pass their property on to their daughters.</li><li>Daughters would be able to inherit property and retain their father's name.</li><li>If a man died and had no living son or daughter, his property would be passed on to his brothers or his uncles or to his nearest relative. The property would always remain in the family.</li></ul>

3. What did you think about the daughters of Zelophehad, and what did the Holy Spirit teach you through their example about the right way to handle problems—especially problems dealing with injustice.

reflect

Personal application; answers will vary.

Day Four

pray

1. Today you'll be studying the power of the spoken word. Before you begin, pray and commit to speak life-giving, refreshing words to every person whose life will intersect yours today.

   A person's words can be life giving water;
   words of true wisdom are as refreshing as a bubbling brook.
   —Proverbs 18:4

Back in Week One, you learned about 3C Syndrome, a malady marked by Contentiousness, Crabbiness, and frequent bouts of Complaining—all of the primary symptoms of the Irritating Woman. 3C is easily identified and, as we've learned, all women struggle with it. But men are not immune from it either. Remember Aaron, Moses' brother? He had a pretty bad case of 3C himself.

This week you've discovered:

- The dangers of 3C: destroyed relationships and God's judgment.

- The source of 3C: the sin of your ancestors, Adam and Eve.

- The root causes of 3C: the desire to control others, as well as jealousy, ambition, envy, etc.

Our goal today is to discover the cure for 3C. Yes, hallelujah, there is a cure! It's easily administered, available to everyone, and it can completely reverse the adverse effects of 3C. What is this miraculous remedy? It's something I call 3B. Curious about this cure-all? C'mon, let's get in the Word and get more info.

2. Read Ephesians 4:29.

> *Let no unwholesome word proceed from your mouth,*
> *but only such a word as is good for edification,*
> *according to the need of the moment, that it may give*
> *grace to those who hear.*
>
> —Ephesians 4:29 *NASB*

3. According to Ephesians 4:29, what are the only kind of words you are allowed to speak? Circle the answer in the verse.

Ephesians 4:29 gives us three divine boundaries for every word we speak. First, we must choose words that are "good" (*agathos* in the Greek), which is defined as "benevolent and beneficial."[6] Second, our words must "edify" (*oikodome* in the Greek), which means to "build up and spiritually profit" others.[7] The final criteria for the words we choose is that they must "give grace" (*charis* in the Greek), which means to bless and benefit others.[8]

In Dr. Spiros Zodhiates's wonderful resource, *The Complete Word Study Dictionary New Testament*, he defines grace like this:

A favor done without expectation of return; the absolutely free expression of the loving kindness of God to men finding its only motive in the bounty and benevolence of the Giver; unearned and unmerited favor.[9]

What does all of this mean to us? Very simply, it means that the words that flow from our lips must do three things: **build**, **bless**, and **benefit**. This is 3B speech—the cure for 3C. Furthermore, we're to speak these words in a way that illustrates and emulates God's grace, which means even if the hearer has not earned and does not deserve to hear 3B words, we must speak them anyway.

Do these boundaries mean that we cannot confront or correct others or honestly express ourselves to them? Absolutely not, but it does mean that we must do it in a positive, gracious way with the motivation of building up, not tearing down.

4. What do 3B words look and sound like? To discover practical examples of the specific kinds of words that build, bless, and benefit, let's return to Proverbs for a little lesson on "How to Speak 3B." Read each verse and complete the sentences. To help you get started, I've completed the first one for you.

How to Speak 3B	
Proverbs 10:11 *(NLT)* "The words of the godly are a life-giving fountain; the words of the wicked conceal violent intentions."	*3B words…* *give life to others*
Proverbs 10:21, 12:25 10:21 *(NLT)* "The words of the godly encourage many, but fools are destroyed by their lack of common sense." 12:25 (NLT) "Worry weighs a person down; an encouraging word cheers a person up."	*3B words…* encourage and cheer people up.
Proverbs 10:31–32 *(NLT)* "The mouth of the godly person gives wise advice, but the tongue that deceives will be cut off. The lips of the godly speak helpful words, but the mouth of the wicked speaks perverse words."	*3B words…* give wise advice and helpful words to others.
Proverbs 15:1 *(NLT)* "A gentle answer deflects anger, but harsh words make tempers flare."	*3B words…* give gentle answers that deflect (avert, prevent) anger.
Proverbs 16:23 *(NLT)* "From a wise mind comes wise speech; the words of the wise are persuasive."	*3B words…* reveal wisdom and persuade others.

5. Make a list below of the primary people your life touches on a daily basis, then take each name before the Lord in prayer. Ask Him to show you how you can speak 3B to each of them in the specific way they need to hear it. Ask God to give you sensitivity and discernment to their needs. Confess, repent, and commit to turn away from 3C speech and become a woman who only speaks one language: 3B, words that build, bless, and benefit.

Personal application; answers will vary.

6. How has God spoken to your heart today?

reflect

{

Personal application; answers will vary.

_____

_____

_____

_____

Day Five

pray

{

1. How important is wisdom? Read today's proverb, and commit to seek and apply God's wisdom to your life as though your very life depended on it…because it does.

> *"Whoever finds me (wisdom) finds life and*
> *wins approval from the Lord.*
> *But those who miss me have injured themselves."*
> —Proverbs 8:35–36

I had a reality check at the mall one day. The cell phone of a woman who was shopping just a few feet away from me rang, and she answered it like this, "Where the _____ are you!!" I have no idea how the caller responded, but the woman's loud, profane rant continued for about a minute.

When she hung up, she stashed the phone back into her purse and went right back to her shopping—as though the phone had never rung. I was rattled by the reality of such a public explosion of profanity. But not her. She was less than three feet from me (she knew I had heard her) and she never said a single, "Sorry."

Now let me ask you a question: Who do you think was on the other end of that cell phone? Who do you think that Irritating Woman was talking to? People don't talk to their friends like that, do they? They wouldn't have any friends if they did. I think you and I both know who was on the other end of that cell phone. It was probably a member of that woman's own family – her husband or, perhaps, her child. It still sickens me when I think about that.

Too many teens are growing up in homes where words of death are spoken on a daily basis. How I pray that's not true of your home. But even if it is, precious girl, you cannot compromise or conform to the common standards of our culture. Your family members, friends, teachers—even the people who overhear your cell phone conversations and read your texts—should be the beneficiaries of your grace-filled words.

The principles you'll be learning from God's Word today will build on what you learned yesterday about 3B speech. As you embrace and apply these truths to your life, you'll not only build, bless, and benefit others, you'll become a powerful witness for Christ through your biblically beautiful speech.

2. Irritating Women tend to turn up the volume—and the attitude—when they speak. Read 1 Peter 3:1–4, and record what you learn about the spirit (attitude) and sound (volume) of a biblically beautiful girl.

NOTE: The instructions in 1 Peter 3:1-2 are directed specifically at wives, but the principles in these verses also may be applied to other relationships (for example: your relationship with your parents and others who are in positions of authority over you).

> *(NLT)* [1] "In the same way, you wives must accept the authority of your husbands. Then, even if some refuse to obey the Good News, your godly lives will speak to them without any words. They will be won over [2] by observing your pure and reverent lives. [3] Don't be concerned about the outward beauty of fancy hairstyles, expensive jewelry, or beautiful clothes. [4] You should clothe yourselves instead with the beauty that comes from within, the unfading beauty of a gentle and quiet spirit, which is so precious to God."

- She accepts (submits to) the authority of others God has placed over her.
- Even when those in authority disobey God, she doesn't.
- She is reverent and respectful in her behavior and attitude.
- She is gentle and quiet – she's not a loud mouth.
- She wins others over by her behavior.

3. Profanity, cursing, and cussing. You hear it everywhere: in conversations between girls (or guys) and their friends, in the lyrics of songs, on TV shows, and in movies. The culture doesn't seem to think there's anything profane about profanity, and even Christians are becoming more and more desensitized to it. But let's see what God's unchanging Word says about cussing and cursing. Read the following passage from James, and record what you learn about the tongue (the words you speak) and profanity:

James 3:6-12

> ⁶ *And the tongue is a flame of fire. It is a whole world of wickedness, corrupting your entire body. It can set your whole life on fire, for it is set on fire by hell itself.*
> ⁷ *People can tame all kinds of animals, birds, reptiles, and fish,*
> ⁸ *but no one can tame the tongue. It is restless and evil, full of deadly poison.*
> ⁹ *Sometimes it praises our Lord and Father, and sometimes it curses those who have been made in the image of God.*
> ¹⁰ *And so blessing and cursing come pouring out of the same mouth. Surely, my brothers and sisters, this is not right!*
> ¹¹ *Does a spring of water bubble out with both fresh water and bitter water?*
> ¹² *Does a fig tree produce olives, or a grapevine produce figs? No, and you can't draw fresh water from a salty spring.*

- The tongue is like a flame that sets fires.
- Profanity and wicked words corrupt our entire body.
- The tongue/our words have the power to destroy our lives.
- The tongue cannot be tamed like an animal can.
- The tongue is restless, evil, and full of deadly poison – it can hurt and destroy others.
- The tongue and our words have the potential for both good (praising God) and evil (cursing others).
- It's not right for Christians to use their words for both blessing and cursing (which includes profanity).

4. I have a few super practical scriptures for you to look up. These verses contain some great "talking points"—wisdom and instructions to help you in your everyday conversation. Read each verse on the following chart, and briefly record the truth it teaches about talkin'.

Talking Points: Tips For Talkin'	
Proverbs 10:19 *(NLT)* "Too much talk leads to sin. Be sensible and keep your mouth shut."	Talking too much often leads to sin; those who are wise know when to stop talking and keep their mouths shut.
Proverbs 15:4 *(NLT)* "Gentle words are a tree of life; a deceitful tongue crushes the spirit."	Soft, gentle words bring life to others, but deceitful, lying words crush and hurt others.
Proverbs 15:23, 25:11 15:23 *(NLT)* "Everyone enjoys a fitting reply; it is wonderful to say the right thing at the right time!" 25:11 *(NLT)* "Timely advice is lovely, like golden apples in a silver basket."	Everyone likes those who: 1) say just the right thing at just the right time, and 2) give sound, timely advice.
Proverbs 15:28 *(NLT)* "The heart of the godly thinks carefully before speaking; the mouth of the wicked overflows with evil words."	Godly people think carefully before saying anything.
Proverbs 17:14, 20:3 17:14 *(NLT)* "Starting a quarrel is like opening a floodgate, so stop before a dispute breaks out." 20:3 *(NLT)* "Avoiding a fight is a mark of honor; only fools insist on quarreling."	Starting a quarrel is like breaking a dam – something only a fool would do. Wise people avoid fighting and arguing.
Proverbs 17:27 *(NLT)* "A truly wise person uses few words; a person with understanding is even-tempered."	Those who are truly wise, use few words – they don't wear people out droning on and on. They also are even-tempered – not drama mamas.

5. Before you do your weekly journal assignment, I want you to read one final scripture that was written just for you. After you read it, describe what God is saying specifically to you, a teenage girl, about your life and the words you speak.

Don't let anyone think less of you because you are young.
Be an example to all believers in what you say,
in the way you live, in your love, your faith, and your purity.
—1 Timothy 4:12

6. What has the Lord taught you this week, and how have you seen Him at work in your life? Journal your thoughts by completing the following sentence:

reflect

This week the Lord... _____

| Personal application; answers will vary. |

_____

_____

More than any other single group of women on the planet, mothers-in-law rank number one on the Irritating Woman list—and I have officially joined their ranks. It was a role I felt some degree of dread about. I longed for a mother-in-law mentor—until I realized I already had one: my own precious mother-in-law, Frances Cole.

Fran is the model mother-in-law. She's supportive but not smothering. She's interested but not meddlesome. She's strong but not overbearing. And she's sweet, sweet, sweet. Although many miles separate us, and our times together are too far and few between, her welcome mat is always out and her smile outlasts our stay.

Annie Chapman wrote a wonderful book for mothers-in-law entitled *"The Mother-in-Law Dance."* In one chapter she refers to Proverbs 10:19 (one of the verses you just studied), and she says that for mothers-in-law, "Keeping our words to a minimum is one of the smartest ways to stay out of trouble. In fact, most any response that needs to be addressed can be summed up with three individual words. Those words are "sure," "really," and "wow.""[10]

When Bill and I were 23 and our first son was a tiny baby, we bought a 40-foot travel trailer and went on the road in evangelism. We traveled from church to church and sang for revivals and evangelistic meetings. We lived on love offerings, and we trusted God to pay our bills and keep us fed. When I think about what I might do if one of my children did that today, I hope and pray I'd do just what Fran did—say, "Wow," and little else. Fran must have been worried about us...but we never knew it. Instead, she kept her concerns to herself and prayed for us often.

The term "mother-in-law" has historically been associated with adjectives like "aggravating," "troublemaking," "exasperating," and sometimes even "infuriating." But Frances Cole is a biblically beautiful woman who has shattered the stereotypical mother-in-law mold. And these days, I'm working very hard to follow in her footsteps.

Week Four • *How's That Irritating Woman Working for You?*

The Irritating Woman:

1. Outward signs: * *contentious*, quarrelsome; hard to get along with
   * *mean* and manipulating
   * *pouts*, pleads and nags
   * demanding and *bossy / controlling*

2. Inward issues: A desire to *rule* and *control* others.

How's that Irritating Woman working for you?

1. *Miriam's* Story. It didn't work for her at all! *Num. 12:1–15*

2. *Michal's* Story. It didn't work for her either! *2 Sam. 6:12–23*

What will work for you?

1. The Example of the Daughters of Zelophehad: *Num. 27:1–10*

   a. They took their *problem* to those in *authority*.

   b. They stated their case *simply*, *factually*, and respectfully.

   c. They offered a simple, fair *solution*.

   d. They *entrusted* the *results* to the authorities.

   RESULTS:

   They received what they needed *and* *helped others*, too.

2. The Example of *Acsah* *Joshua 15:13–19*

3. Speaking *3B*: *Ephesians 4:29*

   a. A biblically beautiful young woman speaks *fluent* 3B.

   b. 3B words *build*, *bless*, and *benefit* others.

Week 5 · *The Captivating Woman*

Can a biblically beautiful woman be sensual, sexual, and even seductive? Yes, BUT only if she's married. Proverbs describes a wife like this as "captivating," which means that she's the kind of wife whose husband is crazy in love with her. And if you get married someday, God wants you to be a Captivating Woman.

But what about now? Before you marry. Is it possible to be a Captivating Young Woman? Absolutely! Of course, that doesn't give you a green light to be sensual, sexual, or seductive (that's an Immoral Woman, remember), but you can become the kind of exceptional young woman that guys find very attractive.

This week, you'll discover the biblically beautiful qualities of the Captivating Young Woman. She's not a flirt. She's not a flatterer. And she's not a flaunter (as in itty-bitty shorts and bosom-baring shirts). But she can still attract a guy. And not just any guy. God's Guy. The kind of guy you'll definitely want to date and marry someday, which brings me to another topic you'll be studying this week: how to know if A Guy is God's Guy, or just another cutie-pie.

Precious girl, the principles you will learn this week are so important. Your decision to spend time studying God's Word is critical. So here's a little motivation to help you give this lesson your best effort yet. Every time you sit down to do your homework just think: one day your guy—God's Guy—will be so glad you did. And who knows? He might be a real cutie-pie, too.

Day One

pray

1. Want to be prized, honored, and valued as a young woman? Then seek wisdom. Those who prize her will also be rewarded by her. Begin this week's lesson by praying and asking God to give you wisdom in every area of your life—including your dating and future married life.

> *If you prize wisdom, she will exalt you.*
> *Embrace her and she will honor you.*
> *She will place a lovely wreath on your head;*
> *she will present you with a beautiful crown.*
> —Proverbs 4:8–9

You met the **Captivating Woman** in your first week of this study. As you briefly renew your acquaintance with her today, remember: God included the Captivating Woman in His Word as a role model for your future relationship with your husband.

2. Read the beautiful description of the Captivating Woman:

> ¹⁸ *Let your wife be a fountain of blessing for you.*
> *Rejoice in the wife of your youth.*
> ¹⁹ *She is a loving doe, a graceful deer.*
> *Let her breasts satisfy you always.*
> *May you always be captivated by her love.*
>
> —Proverbs 5:18–19

Although you can't be a Captivating Woman until you get married, you can be the kind of girl that guys find fascinating, intriguing, and even get-down-on-one-knee-and-propose irresistible. Today you're going to meet a young woman just like that. Her name is Ruth, and if you want to learn how to become a biblically beautiful, stand-out-in-the-crowd Captivating Young Woman, Ruth's your role model. You're going to love getting to know her this week!

3. Meet Ruth by reading Ruth 1:1–18, 22. As you read, examine her character, her choices, and the decisions she makes.

Ruth 1:1-18, 22

¹ *In the days when the judges ruled in Israel, a severe famine came upon the land. So a man from Bethlehem in Judah left his home and went to live in the country of Moab, taking his wife and two sons with him.*

² *The man's name was Elimelech, and his wife was Naomi. Their two sons were Mahlon and Kilion. They were Ephrathites from Bethlehem in the land of Judah. And when they reached Moab, they settled there.*

³ *Then Elimelech died, and Naomi was left with her two sons.*

⁴ *The two sons married Moabite women. One married a woman named Orpah, and the other a woman named Ruth. But about ten years later,*

⁵ *both Mahlon and Kilion died. This left Naomi alone, without her two sons or her husband.*

⁶ *Then Naomi heard in Moab that the Lord had blessed his people in Judah by giving them good crops again. So Naomi and her daughters-in-law got ready to leave Moab to return to her homeland.*

⁷ *With her two daughters-in-law she set out from the place where she had been living, and they took the road that would lead them back to Judah.*

⁸ *But on the way, Naomi said to her two daughters-in-law, "Go back to your mothers' homes. And may the Lord reward you for your kindness to your husbands and to me.*

⁹ May the Lord bless you with the security of another marriage." Then she kissed them good-bye, and they all broke down and wept.

¹⁰ "No," they said. "We want to go with you to your people."

¹¹ But Naomi replied, "Why should you go on with me? Can I still give birth to other sons who could grow up to be your husbands?

¹² No, my daughters, return to your parents' homes, for I am too old to marry again. And even if it were possible, and I were to get married tonight and bear sons, then what?

¹³ Would you wait for them to grow up and refuse to marry someone else? No, of course not, my daughters! Things are far more bitter for me than for you, because the Lord himself has raised his fist against me."

¹⁴ And again they wept together, and Orpah kissed her mother-in-law good-bye. But Ruth clung tightly to Naomi.

¹⁵ "Look," Naomi said to her, "your sister-in-law has gone back to her people and to her gods. You should do the same."

¹⁶ But Ruth replied, "Don't ask me to leave you and turn back. Wherever you go, I will go; wherever you live, I will live. Your people will be my people, and your God will be my God.

¹⁷ Wherever you die, I will die, and there I will be buried. May the Lord punish me severely if I allow anything but death to separate us!"

¹⁸ When Naomi saw that Ruth was determined to go with her, she said nothing more…

²² So Naomi returned from Moab, accompanied by her daughter-in-law Ruth, the young Moabite woman. They arrived in Bethlehem in late spring, at the beginning of the barley harvest.

4. Record your answers to the following questions about Ruth:

   a. As a young woman, Ruth experienced an unexpected tragedy. What happened (verses 4–5)?

   > She was married but her husband died. She became a young widow.

b. Naomi, Ruth's mother-in-law, decided to leave Moab and return to her home in Bethlehem. Ruth and Orpah (Ruth's sister) went with Naomi as she started the journey, but what choice did Orpah ultimately make (v. 14–15)?

> Orpah ultimately decided to leave Naomi and Ruth and return to her people and her gods in Moab.

c. What choices did Ruth make (verses 16–17)?

> - Ruth begged Naomi not to ask her to leave.
> - Ruth made a commitment to Naomi to stay with her until death.
> - Ruth also made the decision that Naomi's people (the Israelites) would be her people.
> - Ruth chose to serve and follow God just as Naomi did.

d. Naomi warned Ruth repeatedly about the risks involved in her choices (verses 8–9, 11–13), yet Ruth accepted those risks and stuck with her decision. What does this reveal about Ruth and her character?

> - Ruth was selfless, loving, and loyal.
> - Ruth loved Naomi unconditionally.
> - Ruth was courageous; she left Moab – everything and everyone that was familiar to her – and followed Naomi to a foreign land.

e. What did Ruth's choices reveal about her faith and spirituality?

> - Ruth's choices reveal a deep commitment to follow and serve God.
> - Her choices also reveal her great faith in God; although Ruth basically had nothing and no one to provide for her, she was determined to stay with Naomi and to serve Naomi's God.

5. I realize that you've only just met Ruth, but I wonder: What qualities does she possess that would make her a fantastic friend?

reflect

> Personal application; answers will vary.
>
> _____
>
> _____
>
> _____

Day Two

pray

1. Take a few minutes to love yourself. How? By praying and asking God for wisdom as you study His Word today.

> *To acquire wisdom is to love oneself;*
> *people who cherish understanding will prosper.*
> —Proverbs 19:8

Yesterday, you read Ruth's "back story." She was born and raised in Moab, a land where idolatry and immorality were rampant. Both Ruth and her sister married into an Israelite family (a family that worshipped God) who had moved to Moab from Bethlehem because of a famine. Ruth must have grown to love and respect her new family very much, because when she, her sister, and her mother-in-law all became widows, she chose to move to Bethlehem with her mother-in-law, Naomi.

As a widow, Naomi had very little to offer Ruth, and when they arrived in Bethlehem, they were basically destitute. But it was the beginning of the barley harvest, and Israelite farmers were commanded by God to allow the poor to "glean"—to harvest the edges of the grain fields and to pick up and keep anything the workers dropped.

Today, you'll follow our girl, Ruth, to the harvest fields of Bethlehem where she will meet the man who will ultimately become the love of her life: Boaz. Watch Ruth carefully, and notice how she handles herself. There's so much you can learn from her. But be sure to study Boaz, too, girl, because he's just the kind of guy God's got in mind for you.

2. Get to know Ruth better as you read Ruth 2.

Ruth 2

¹ *Now there was a wealthy and influential man in Bethlehem named Boaz, who was a relative of Naomi's husband, Elimelech.*

² *One day Ruth the Moabite said to Naomi, "Let me go out into the harvest fields to pick up the stalks of grain left behind by anyone who is kind enough to let me do it." Naomi replied, "All right, my daughter, go ahead."*

³ *So Ruth went out to gather grain behind the harvesters. And as it happened, she found herself working in a field that belonged to Boaz, the relative of her father-in-law, Elimelech.*

⁴ *While she was there, Boaz arrived from Bethlehem and greeted the harvesters. "The Lord be with you!" he said. "The Lord bless you!" the harvesters replied.*

⁵ *Then Boaz asked his foreman, "Who is that young woman over there? Who does she belong to?"*

⁶ *And the foreman replied, "She is the young woman from Moab who came back with Naomi.*

⁷ *She asked me this morning if she could gather grain behind the harvesters. She has been hard at work ever since, except for a few minutes' rest in the shelter."*

⁸ *Boaz went over and said to Ruth, "Listen, my daughter. Stay right here with us when you gather grain; don't go to any other fields. Stay right behind the young women working in my field.*

⁹ *See which part of the field they are harvesting, and then follow them. I have warned the young men not to treat you roughly. And when you are thirsty, help yourself to the water they have drawn from the well."*

¹⁰ *Ruth fell at his feet and thanked him warmly. "What have I done to deserve such kindness?" she asked. "I am only a foreigner."*

¹¹ *"Yes, I know," Boaz replied. "But I also know about everything you have done for your mother-in-law since the death of your husband. I have heard how you left your father and mother and your own land to live here among complete strangers.*

¹² *May the Lord, the God of Israel, under whose wings you have come to take refuge, reward you fully for what you have done."*

¹³ *"I hope I continue to please you, sir," she replied. "You have comforted me by speaking so kindly to me, even though I am not one of your workers."*

¹⁴ *At mealtime Boaz called to her, "Come over here, and help yourself to some food. You can dip your bread in the sour wine." So she sat with his harvesters, and Boaz gave her some roasted grain to eat. She ate all she wanted and still had some left over.*

15 When Ruth went back to work again, Boaz ordered his young men, "Let her gather grain right among the sheaves without stopping her.

16 And pull out some heads of barley from the bundles and drop them on purpose for her. Let her pick them up, and don't give her a hard time!"

17 So Ruth gathered barley there all day, and when she beat out the grain that evening, it filled an entire basket.

18 She carried it back into town and showed it to her mother-in-law. Ruth also gave her the roasted grain that was left over from her meal.

19 "Where did you gather all this grain today?" Naomi asked. "Where did you work? May the Lord bless the one who helped you!" So Ruth told her mother-in-law about the man in whose field she had worked. She said, "The man I worked with today is named Boaz."

20 "May the Lord bless him!" Naomi told her daughter-in-law. "He is showing his kindness to us as well as to your dead husband. That man is one of our closest relatives, one of our family redeemers."

21 Then Ruth said, "What's more, Boaz even told me to come back and stay with his harvesters until the entire harvest is completed."

22 "Good!" Naomi exclaimed. "Do as he said, my daughter. Stay with his young women right through the whole harvest. You might be harassed in other fields, but you'll be safe with him."

23 So Ruth worked alongside the women in Boaz's fields and gathered grain with them until the end of the barley harvest. Then she continued working with them through the wheat harvest in early summer. And all the while she lived with her mother-in-law.

3. Record your answers to the following questions:

a. How did Ruth end up in Boaz's field (verses 2-3)? Did she know who he was and purposefully go to his field on a husband-hunting expedition?

> Without any prior knowledge of Boaz, Ruth simply went out one morning to find food for herself and Naomi. She was hungry not husband-hunting. But "as it happened" (v. 3), God led her to the perfect field where she would find food and (unknowingly) her future husband.

b. According to the foreman, what did Ruth do all morning (verse 7), and what does this reveal about her?

> - Ruth arrived at the field early in the day – she didn't "sleep in" which reveals that she was disciplined and eager to work to provide for her and Naomi's needs.
> - She asked permission to gather grain behind the harvesters. She was polite and respectful to those in authority over her.
> - She worked hard in the fields; she was not lazy and she didn't expect others to do the work or provide for her.

c. How did Ruth meet Boaz? Who made the first move (verse 8), and what does this reveal about Ruth?

> Boaz made the first move. Although Ruth had discovered that he was the wealthy land owner and boss (v. 4), she didn't pursue him. This proves that she was not husband-hunting or gold-digging that day.

d. How did Ruth handle herself around Boaz (verses 10 & 13)? Was she a flirt?

> Ruth did not flirt with Boaz like many girls in her position would have done. Instead, she was modest, gracious, respectful, and thankful to Boaz.

e. What kind of reputation did Ruth have (verses 11–12)?

> - Others recognized Ruth as someone who loved and cared for her mother-in-law.
> - They also knew that she and Naomi were both widows.
> - Ruth's reputation was that she had chosen to leave her mother, father, and her homeland to come to Bethlehem and be part of the people of Israel.
> - Ruth's reputation was that she trusted God.

f. What specific things did Boaz do to protect and provide for Ruth (verses 8–9, 14–16, 21)?

> - Boaz told her to stay in his field and not to go to another one.
> - He told her to remain close to the women who worked for him.
> - He warned the young men not to harm or harass her.
> - He provided for her food and water.
> - He instructed his men to purposefully drop gain for her to gather.
> - He invited her to stay with his harvesters throughout the harvest season.

4. In what way is Boaz like the kind of guy you'd like to date or marry (and don't include "rich" ☺)?

reflect

> Personal application; answers will vary.
> _____
> _____
> _____
> _____

Day Three

pray

1. According to today's Proverb, getting wisdom is a priority. Pray and ask God to give you wisdom as you continue to study Ruth and Boaz. Commit to take what He's taught you through their example, and apply it to your life today.

Getting wisdom is the most important thing you can do!
—Proverbs 4:7

We can't know for sure whether or not sparks flew when Ruth and Boaz met, but they certainly seemed to admire one another. Boaz showed his admiration by the affirming words he spoke to Ruth, and Ruth showed her admiration for him by responding to him with honor and respect. I'd say their relationship was off to a really good start, wouldn't you?

Weeks went by as Ruth continued to glean in Boaz's fields, and this gave them the opportunity to observe and get to know one another better. But dating? No, they didn't really date back then. So how will our two lovebirds ever get together? Find out today as the harvest season ends and their commitment to one another begins.

2. Read Ruth 3, an exciting turning point in the story and saga of Ruth.

Ruth 3

¹ One day Naomi said to Ruth, "My daughter, it's time that I found a permanent home for you, so that you will be provided for.

² Boaz is a close relative of ours, and he's been very kind by letting you gather grain with his young women. Tonight he will be winnowing barley at the threshing floor.

³ Now do as I tell you—take a bath and put on perfume and dress in your nicest clothes. Then go to the threshing floor, but don't let Boaz see you until he has finished eating and drinking.

⁴ Be sure to notice where he lies down; then go and uncover his feet and lie down there. He will tell you what to do."

⁵ "I will do everything you say," Ruth replied.

⁶ So she went down to the threshing floor that night and followed the instructions of her mother-in-law.

⁷ After Boaz had finished eating and drinking and was in good spirits, he lay down at the far end of the pile of grain and went to sleep. Then Ruth came quietly, uncovered his feet, and lay down.

⁸ Around midnight Boaz suddenly woke up and turned over. He was surprised to find a woman lying at his feet!

⁹ "Who are you?" he asked. "I am your servant Ruth," she replied. "Spread the corner of your covering over me, for you are my family redeemer."

¹⁰ "The Lord bless you, my daughter!" Boaz exclaimed. "You are showing even more family loyalty now than you did before, for you have not gone after a younger man, whether rich or poor.

¹¹ Now don't worry about a thing, my daughter. I will do what is necessary, for everyone in town knows you are a virtuous woman.

¹² But while it's true that I am one of your family redeemers, there is another man who is more closely related to you than I am.

¹³ Stay here tonight, and in the morning I will talk to him. If he is willing to redeem you, very well. Let him marry you. But if he is not willing, then as surely as the Lord lives, I will redeem you myself! Now lie down here until morning."

¹⁴ So Ruth lay at Boaz's feet until the morning, but she got up before it was light enough for people to recognize each other. For Boaz had said, "No one must know that a woman was here at the threshing floor."

¹⁵ *Then Boaz said to her, "Bring your cloak and spread it out." He measured six scoops of barley into the cloak and placed it on her back. Then he returned to the town.*

¹⁶ *When Ruth went back to her mother-in-law, Naomi asked, "What happened, my daughter?" Ruth told Naomi everything Boaz had done for her,*

¹⁷ *and she added, "He gave me these six scoops of barley and said, 'Don't go back to your mother-in-law empty-handed.'"*

¹⁸ *Then Naomi said to her, "Just be patient, my daughter, until we hear what happens. The man won't rest until he has settled things today."*

3. Record your answers to the following questions:

a. What did Naomi tell Ruth to do and why (verses 1–4)?

> - Because she loved Ruth like a daughter, Naomi wanted to help make sure that Ruth would have a permanent home and a husband who would provide for her.
> - Because Boaz was their relative and had been very kind to Ruth, Naomi instructed her to "take a bath and put on perfume and dress in your nicest clothes." Then Ruth was to go in secret to the threshing floor (where Boaz was working), lie down at his feet when he fell asleep, and do whatever he told her to do when he awoke.

b. Did Ruth do as Naomi told her? Circle the correct answer:

Yes   No

c. If you had been Ruth, would you have followed Naomi's instructions? Circle one of the following answers: Personal application; answers will vary.

No, absolutely not!   Yes, you betcha!   Yikes! I'm not sure

Naomi's instructions to Ruth seem really strange, I know. But keep in mind that Naomi loved Ruth and wanted the very best for her. Plus, she knew that Boaz could redeem Ruth, which meant that he had the legal right to purchase the land that belonged to Elimelech and his sons (Naomi's deceased husband and sons) and marry Ruth.

You may also be wondering why Naomi told Ruth to lie down at Boaz's feet as he slept. Well, according to the customs of that day, by lying at his feet and requesting that Boaz cover her with his garment, Ruth was symbolically asking him to protect her by becoming her redeemer and husband.

It took a lot of faith and courage for Ruth to follow Naomi's instructions. But I think Naomi knew by the way Boaz treated Ruth that he loved her. Plus, Ruth and Naomi were tight. She must have been aware of Ruth's love for Boaz. Sensing that the time was ripe for a commitment, and wanting the very best for her beloved Ruth, God used Naomi to bring Ruth and Boaz together.

Now I want you to consider another very important issue that relates to Ruth Chapter 3. Some guys will tell a girl that they love them—and maybe even want to marry them someday—when all they really want is sex. And some girls will go to bed or even move in with a guy like that. So how can you really know if a guy truly loves you or if he just wants to have sex with you? To answer to that question, let's examine Ruth 3:13–14 again.

4. Read Ruth 3:13–14, and notice the verbal commitment Boaz made to Ruth. How did Ruth know that his words were sincere and that he wasn't just attempting to get her to have sex with him? (verse 14)?

- Because he didn't have sex with her; she remained at his feet all night just as he told her to do.
- Because he could have tried to seduce her, but he didn't.
- Because he was concerned about her reputation; he told her to leave before light so no one would see her.

5. How can you know if a guy really loves you or if you love him? In other words, how can you recognize a love that is true? Read 1 Corinthians 13:4–8, and record what you learn about love by completing the following sentence:

(NLT) [4] "Love is patient and kind. Love is not jealous or boastful or proud [5] or rude. It does not demand its own way. It is not irritable, and it keeps no record of being wronged. [6] It does not rejoice about injustice but rejoices whenever the truth wins out. [7] Love never gives up, never loses faith, is always hopeful, and endures through every circumstance. [8] Prophecy and speaking in unknown languages and special knowledge will become useless. But love will last forever!"

A guy who really loves me will be _____

_____

_____

6. What have you learned today to help you know whether or not a guy is sincere in his love and commitment to you…and you to him?

Personal application; answers will vary.

reflect

_____

_____

_____

Day Four

pray

1. Begin your time of study today by praying and asking God to use the wisdom He is giving you this week to guard and protect your future.

   Don't turn your back on wisdom, for she will protect you.
   Love her, and she will guard you.
   —Proverbs 4:6

I hope the real-life love story of Ruth and Boaz has inspired and encouraged you this week. But most of all, I hope you know that God cares for you every bit as much as He cared for Ruth. He has incredible plans for you, so do not settle for anything less than His best as you date and, perhaps, marry.

When Ruth made the choice to leave her old life behind and follow Naomi and God by faith, she probably never dreamed God had such amazing plans in store for her. Precious girl, be a modern-day Ruth. Follow God and His path for your life no matter what the risks or costs may be. And as you read the happy ending of Ruth's story today, know this: God promises to reward all—and that includes you—who seek Him (Hebrews 11:6).

2. Read Ruth 4:1–13.

Ruth 4:1-13

1 *Boaz went to the town gate and took a seat there. Just then the family redeemer he had mentioned came by, so Boaz called out to him, "Come over here and sit down, friend. I want to talk to you." So they sat down together.*
2 *Then Boaz called ten leaders from the town and asked them to sit as witnesses.*
3 *And Boaz said to the family redeemer, "You know Naomi, who came back from Moab. She is selling the land that belonged to our relative Elimelech.*
4 *I thought I should speak to you about it so that you can redeem it if you wish. If you want the land, then buy it here in the presence of these witnesses. But if you don't want it, let me know right away, because I am next in line to redeem it after you." The man replied, "All right, I'll redeem it."*

⁵ Then Boaz told him, *"Of course, your purchase of the land from Naomi also requires that you marry Ruth, the Moabite widow. That way she can have children who will carry on her husband's name and keep the land in the family."*

⁶ *"Then I can't redeem it,"* the family redeemer replied, *"because this might endanger my own estate. You redeem the land; I cannot do it."*

⁷ Now in those days it was the custom in Israel for anyone transferring a right of purchase to remove his sandal and hand it to the other party. This publicly validated the transaction.

⁸ So the other family redeemer drew off his sandal as he said to Boaz, *"You buy the land."*

⁹ Then Boaz said to the elders and to the crowd standing around, *"You are witnesses that today I have bought from Naomi all the property of Elimelech, Kilion, and Mahlon.*

¹⁰ *And with the land I have acquired Ruth, the Moabite widow of Mahlon, to be my wife. This way she can have a son to carry on the family name of her dead husband and to inherit the family property here in his hometown. You are all witnesses today."*

¹¹ Then the elders and all the people standing in the gate replied, *"We are witnesses! May the Lord make this woman who is coming into your home like Rachel and Leah, from whom all the nation of Israel descended! May you prosper in Ephrathah and be famous in Bethlehem.*

¹² *And may the Lord give you descendants by this young woman who will be like those of our ancestor Perez, the son of Tamar and Judah."*

¹³ So Boaz took Ruth into his home, and she became his wife. When he slept with her, the Lord enabled her to become pregnant, and she gave birth to a son.

3. Record your answers to the following questions:

   a. In Ruth 3:13, Boaz promised Ruth that he would do everything within his power to redeem and marry her. According to what you just read, how did Boaz fulfill his promise (verses 1–8)?

   > - Boaz did not delay; he went that same morning to work things out.
   > - Boaz talked to the other man – the closest family redeemer – to find out if he was interested in redeeming Elimelech's land and marrying Ruth.
   > - As soon as the closest relative bowed out, Boaz made it known publicly that he would become the redeemer.
   > - Boaz was a man of his word.

b. Put yourself in Ruth's shoes. How do you think she felt when she heard about the way Boaz had publicly proclaimed his desire and intention to marry her?

> •   The news had to have made her happy and grateful.
> •   It probably made her love and respect for Boaz grow even deeper.
> •   It probably affirmed her of his love and respect for her.

c. How did God bless Ruth and Boaz (verse 13)?

> After they married, God enabled them to have a son.

4. Think back to the first chapter of Ruth and the way Ruth's story begins. Now fast forward to Ruth 4 and the way Ruth's story ends. As you consider these two very different chapters of the same book, answer the following questions:

a. What did you learn about the importance of making good choices even when it's hard and it seems risky?

> •   God always blesses those who follow Him by faith.
> •   The choices we make in the difficult days and crossroads moments of our lives, are often far more important than we realize.

b. Why do you think God recorded the beautiful love story of Ruth and Boaz in the Bible? What is He saying to you today?

> There are many possible answers and applications for this question such as:
> •   To give us a role model (Ruth) and example to follow in our relationships with guys.
> •   To give us a role model (Boaz) and example of the kind of guy God wants us to date and marry.
> •   To show us that God wants the very best for all of His children.

5. What characteristic in Ruth's life do you most desire in yours? Explain your answer.

reflect

Personal application; answers will vary.

Day Five

pray

1. Embracing the culture's beliefs (or even our own personal opinions) about dating, sex, and marriage is very dangerous. Before you begin your final day of study this week, spend a few minutes in prayer. Commit to embrace the wisdom and truth God has shown you through your study of Ruth.

Trusting oneself is foolish, but those who walk in wisdom are safe.
—Proverbs 28:26

Today you will discover God's #1 requirement for any guy you date. It is the most important quality you should look for in any potential date. Why? Because A Guy you date will eventually become The Guy you marry. But before you find out what God's #1 requirement is, spend a few minutes reflecting upon the story of Ruth and Boaz.

2. Recall and review the story of Ruth and Boaz. As you picture each chapter in your mind, record on the following chart several reasons why you think Ruth and Boaz were attracted to one another.

I think Ruth was attracted to Boaz because...	I think Boaz was attracted to Ruth because...
• He was respected by those who worked for him. • She knew he was a spiritual and godly man. • Time and time again, he was kind to her and Naomi. • He protected her; she felt safe working for him and being with him. • He was thoughtful and generous; he made sure she and Naomi always had enough food. • He did not take advantage of her when he could have.	• She was humble, hard-working, and modest. • She had a good reputation with others. • She was loyal, kind, and loving to Naomi. • She was respectful of him. • She wasn't a flirt. • She could have gone after a younger man (3:10), but she chose him instead.

Precious girl, I hope your study of Ruth will enable you to recognize a Boaz, the kind of guy God has in mind for you. Yes, he is rare, but he's out there, so be patient. Follow God (like Ruth did), and if His plans for your life include marriage, He'll lead you to your Boaz. And never ever settle for a Bozo!

Bozo is the counterfeit version (evil twin) of Boaz. Unlike Boaz, Bozo won't protect you (or your purity), and he won't provide for you either. That's because Bozo is a taker, not a giver. He's also a talker—as in "sweet talker." Honey, Bozo will promise you the moon, but he's all talk and no commitment. Do not waste your time, and do not give your heart to Bozo— he'll just take it and break it.

One of the primary ways you can know whether or not a guy is a Boaz or a Bozo is by making sure he meets God's #1 requirement for any guy that you date. Discover that essential, foremost requirement right now.

3. Read 2 Corinthians 6:14 (I'm giving it to you in two translations), and record in your own words God's #1 requirement for any guy that you date.

2 Corinthians 6:14 *(NIV)*

Do not be yoked together with unbelievers.
For what do righteousness and wickedness have in common?
Or what fellowship can light have with darkness?

2 Corinthians 6:14

Don't team up with those who are unbelievers.
How can righteousness be a partner with wickedness?
How can light live with darkness?

God's #1 requirement for any guy that I date is:

that he be a true Christian.

So, how can you know if a guy meets this requirement? Well, before you go out with him, you're going to have to talk to him and ask him some very important questions like, "What do you believe about God, Jesus, and the Bible?" And you absolutely have to ask him, "Are you a Christian?" If he's wishy-washy, or if his answers are unbiblical, then you know you can't "team up" with him. To be succinct, you cannot date him (and if you do, you'll be making a choice that is in direct disobedience to God—a dangerous thing to do).

But even if he answers every question correctly and tells you that he's a Christian, there's still one more thing you need to do before you can go out with him...and you're about to find out what that is.

4. Read Matthew 7:16–23 and Galatians 5:22–23, then answer the questions that follow.

Matthew 7:16–23

You can identify [people] by their fruit, that is, by the way they act. Can you pick grapes from thornbushes, or figs from thistles? A good tree produces good fruit, and a bad tree produces bad fruit. A good tree can't produce bad fruit, and a bad tree can't produce good fruit…Yes, just as you can identify a tree by its fruit, so you can identify people by their actions. Not everyone who calls out to me, "Lord! Lord!" will enter the Kingdom of Heaven. Only those who actually do the will of my Father in heaven will enter. On judgment day many will say to me, "Lord! Lord! We prophesied in your name and cast out demons in your name and performed many miracles in your name." But I will reply, "I never knew you. Get away from me, you who break God's laws."

Galatians 5:22–23

But the Holy Spirit produces this kind of fruit in our lives: love, joy, peace, patience, kindness, goodness, faithfulness, gentleness, and self-control.

a. According to Matthew 7:16–21, how can you identify what kind of person somebody is?

> - You look at the fruit of their life – the way they act and live.
> - People are what they do. If they're good, their lives will produce good fruit. But if they're bad, their lives will produce bad fruit.
> - People (or a guy) may say or believe that they are Christians; but if they truly are, there will be evidence.

b. According to Galatians 5:22–23, how can you know if a guy (or anyone else) is a Christian?

> You observe their life to see if the Holy Spirit is producing the spiritual fruit of love, joy, peace, patience, kindness, goodness, faithfulness, gentleness, and self-control in their lives.

    c. So, before you "team up" and date (or marry) a guy, what should you do?

> • You need to observe him carefully until you can see the way he consistently acts, speaks, and lives.
> • You need to be cautious – what he says about his own spiritual life may or may not be true.
> • You need to be able to see the consistent fruit of the Holy Spirit in his life.

5. What kind of guy do you want to say, "I do," to? What traits and characteristics do you want him to possess? Consider these questions and everything you've learned this week, then make a list of these qualities by completing the following sentence:

If I ever get married, I want my husband to be...

> Personal application; answers will vary.

       I want to encourage you to make a copy of that list, and keep it somewhere handy. Use it often as you pray asking God to build each specific characteristic into your future husband's heart and life. And as you prepare to date, you can also use your list as a standard to help guide you to God's guy.

6. How has the Lord encouraged and spoken to your heart this week? What specific actions is He leading you to take in response to what He's taught you? Conclude your week of study by taking a couple of minutes to journal your answers to these questions.

reflect

> *This week the Lord...* _____
>
> Personal application; answers will vary.
>
> _____
>
> _____

She was a beautiful little girl when she learned a very ugly truth: some men are predators, not protectors. Used and abused, she longed to be loved. But in her pursuit for love, she became a statistic instead: a pregnant teen.

A few years later, she moved to Houston seeking a new start. Soon, she met a man who vowed to love, honor, and cherish her. But unfaithfulness tore their marriage apart, and she was left with two small children and no one to protect and provide for her or them.

With a pain-filled past and a frightening future before her, she sought love from the only One she had left: God. And He lavished His love upon her. He taught her what true love really is. He became her Protector and her Provider. And as her confidence and security in His love for her grew, He even healed the wounds from her childhood.

I met her at church. Her name was Christy, and we became friends. Her love for God and hunger to grow in His Word was stunning. As I got to know her and her two little boys, I became an eyewitness to the miraculous way that God can be a Husband to the husbandless and a Father to the fatherless.

Christy remained a single mom for several years. But one day, after reading the Book of Ruth, she whispered a bold, brief prayer: "Lord, I know You can do for me what You did for Ruth. Please, God, bring me a Boaz." And He did! Now my beloved friend, Christy, is the captivating wife of David Simmons, a loving, giving, godly man.

Precious girl, be a Ruth. Be a Christy. Pursue God, not guys, because that's what will transform and enable you to become a Captivating Young Woman. Then don't be surprised when God brings a Boaz your way. He delights in doing things like that for girls like Ruth. And Christy. And you.

Week Five • *How a Godly Girl Attracts a Godly Guy*

<u>Step 1</u>: **Embrace God's <u>*standard*</u> as your <u>*standard*</u>; only date / marry a Christian.**

> *"Don't team up with those who are unbelievers. How can righteousness be a partner with wickedness? How can light live with darkness?"*
> —2 Corinthians 6:14 *NLT*

<u>Step 2</u>: **Follow Ruth's example; become a <u>*captivating*</u> young woman.**

1) Give God <u>*priority*</u> in your life. *Ruth 1:16, Psalm 37:3–6*

2) <u>*Earn*</u> the <u>*respect*</u> of others by:
   * your virtuous <u>*character*</u> *Ruth 2:10–13, Psalm 37:6*
   * your willingness to <u>*work*</u> *Ruth 2:2–3, 6–7*

3) Take care of your <u>*physical appearance*</u>. *Ruth 3:3*

4) Do not compromise your <u>*sexual purity*</u>. *Ruth 2–3*

5) Let your desire for a <u>*commitment*</u> to <u>*marry*</u> be known. *Ruth 3:6–9*

<u>Step 3</u>: **Learn to <u>*recognize*</u> a godly guy.**

1) He will give God <u>*priority*</u> in his life. *Ruth 2:4, 8–15*

2) He will be <u>*respected*</u> by others.

3) He will <u>*protect*</u> you. *Ruth 2:8, 15*

4) He will <u>*provide*</u> for you. *Ruth 2:8–9, 14–16*

5) He will make a <u>*commitment*</u> to you and will <u>*publicly*</u> follow through with it. *Ruth 3:11–4:10*

Week 6 • *The Ideal Woman*

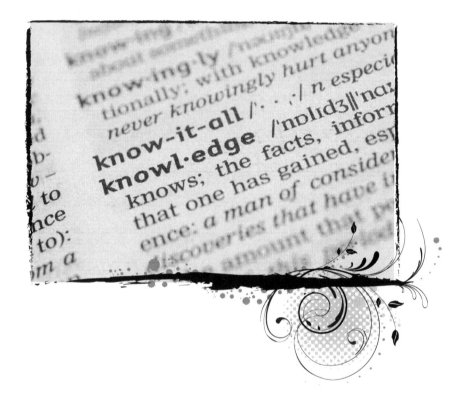

Dessert has always been my favorite course—even if it's just a couple of Oreos after a peanut butter and banana sandwich. Some say, "Life's short—eat dessert first." But not me. I like saving the best for last. And that's exactly how I feel about this final lesson on Beauty Do #2, the Ideal Woman. Of all the women presented in Proverbs, she's the best, so she is saved as the final and most satisfying course.

Now don't get the wrong idea. The Ideal Woman is no fancy cream puff or sugar-filled bonbon. She's a woman of substance. She leads a purposeful and significant life. Although she wears many hats and juggles numerous responsibilities, she balances the various aspects of her life with wisdom, integrity, and lots of love. Girl, she's the kind of woman God wants you to become.

While I was writing the first *Beauty by The Book* study (the one for adult women), one of my favorite friends called to encourage me. She said, "I really like that you used the word 'becoming' in the subtitle of the study—I like that word. It reminds me that biblical beauty is a process." To be honest, I hadn't even considered that, but I was so grateful God revealed it to her and led her to share it with me.

Biblical beauty is, indeed, a process. So don't be intimidated by the **Ideal Woman** this week—even she had to go through the process of "becoming." And if she made it, girl, you can, too. Here's to "becoming."

Day One

1. If you're a sugar addict like I am, you're going to love today's proverb! Read it, then pray and ask God to make this week's lesson a sweet treat and a delicious dessert of wisdom from His Word.

> *My child, eat honey, for it is good,*
> *and the honeycomb is sweet to the taste.*
> *In the same way, wisdom is sweet to your soul.*
> *If you find it, you will have a bright future,*
> *and your hopes will not be cut short.*
> —Proverbs 24:13–14

As I was preparing this final lesson of our study and thinking about you, the Lord brought a specific passage to my heart. Take a look:

> *Older women must train the younger women to love their husbands and*
> *their children, to live wisely and be pure, to work in their homes,*
> *to do good, and to be submissive to their husbands.*
> *Then they will not bring shame on the word of God.*
> —Titus 2:4–5

Titus 2:4-5 instructs older women, like me, to train younger women, like you. It even includes a list of the specific things I'm supposed to teach you: to love your future husband and children, to live wisely and be pure, to work in your home, and to do good (yes, it also includes teaching you to be submissive to your own husband, but since we studied that in Week 4, we won't cover that topic this week). And I'm very excited because the woman we will be studying this week—the Ideal Woman—embodies everything in that list.

Before we begin our Titus 2 training, I want you to know that even if you never marry, you can (and should) become an Ideal Woman. Why? Because she is a role model for all women young and old, single and married. Although I will be using the Ideal Woman to teach you the Titus 2 curriculum and prepare you for marriage and a family someday, the strengths and characteristics of the Ideal Woman will apply to your life today and to your future whether or not you marry. So with that said, let's begin our Titus 2 training by studying a biblical beauty par excellence: the Ideal Woman

2. Find out about the Ideal Woman and her husband by reading the following scriptures from Proverbs 31:

> *Who can find a virtuous and capable wife?*
> *She is worth more than precious rubies. Her husband can trust her,*
> *and she will greatly enrich his life.*
> *She will not hinder him but help him all of her life.*
> —Proverbs 31:10–12

> *Her husband is well known, for he sits*
> *in the council meeting with the other civic leaders.*
> —Proverbs 31:23

> *Her husband praises her: "There are many virtuous and*
> *capable women in the world, but you surpass them all!"*
> —Proverbs 31:28b-29

3. The very first characteristic you learn about the Ideal Woman is that she's trustworthy. Think about that as you answer the following questions:

a. What's so important about being trustworthy? Is it essential for a strong relationship? Why or why not?

> Answers will vary but may include the following:
> *   Trust is the foundation for every lasting relationship.
> *   It's important because it means that someone is worthy of being trusted; they are dependable, honest, and true.
> *   A lack of trust weakens and divides relationships.

b. Why is trust especially important between a husband and wife?

> Answers will vary but may include the following:
> - Because marriage is a covenant relationship between two people witnessed by God. A lack of trust can break and potentially even sever that covenant.
> - Without trust, two (a husband and wife) cannot truly be one (Gen. 2:24).
> - Because of the tension it creates within the home, children often suffer the consequences of their parent's lack of trust for one another.

c. When you marry, what are some things you can do to earn your husband's trust? For example, you could choose not to text, call, or chat online with any of your former boyfriends. Excluding those examples, what other things can you do (or maybe not do) to earn your husband's trust?

> Answers will vary but may include the following:
> - Refrain from speaking negatively about him to him or to others.
> - Treat him with respect.
> - Never flirt with other men – only him.
> - Be honest and responsible with your finances and spending habits.
> - Don't keep secrets from him; be open and honest.
> - Be willing to share your computer, phone, online passwords, and other information with him.
> - Give him priority over every other earthly relationship.

d. Are you trustworthy? What can you do today to become a young woman that others trust?

> Answers will vary but may include the following:
> - Be honest, dependable, and reliable.
> - Refrain from gossiping.
> - Keep your word and your promises.

4. The Ideal Woman helps her husband and enriches his life (verses 10–12). Record some practical ways a wife can help her husband and enrich his life.

> Answers will vary but may include the following:
> - She can encourage and praise him.
> - She can be a source of wise counsel.
> - She can assist and be his helper (Gen. 2:18) in many different ways. For example: projects around the house; shopping and helping him dress well; helping him become successful in his career, etc.
> - By providing a peaceful and positive atmosphere at home.
> - By treating him with respect especially in front of their children.

5. Although the word "love" is never used in the verses you just read from Proverbs 31, how do you know that the Ideal Woman loves her husband?

> • Because she demonstrates her love through her virtuous character.
> • Because she demonstrates her love through her actions – she helps him.
> • She doesn't just say she loves him, she shows and proves it.

6. What are some non-verbal ways you can communicate your love to your family and friends today?

reflect

> Personal application; answers will vary.
>
> _____
>
> _____
>
> _____

Day Two

pray

1. Wisdom enables us to build our homes and to build up the people we love. Ask God to give you wisdom to build the home and family you live with today, and the home you may share with your future husband and children someday.

   A wise woman builds her home,
   but a foolish woman tears it down
   with her own hands.
   —Proverbs 14:1

Yesterday we began our Titus 2 older woman/younger woman training session, and you learned how to love your future husband. Today's lesson will teach you some very practical ways you can love your future children.

Your role model this week is our fifth and final female from Proverbs: The Ideal Woman. As you study her relationship with her kids, I'm praying that she will inspire you to become a mom just like her someday.

2. Find out about the Ideal Woman and her responsibilities and relationship with her children by reading the following verses:

> *She gets up before dawn to prepare breakfast for her household.*
> —Proverbs 31:15

> *She has no fear of winter for her household,*
> *for everyone has warm clothes.*
> —Proverbs 31:21

> *When she speaks, her words are wise,*
> *and she gives instructions with kindness.*
> *She carefully watches everything in her household*
> *and suffers nothing from laziness.*
> *Her children stand and bless her.*
> —Proverbs 31:26–28

3. According to Proverbs 31:15, 21, 26-28, what are some of the specific ways the Ideal Woman takes care of her children?

- She cooks and prepares their meals.
- She makes sure they have the clothes, coats, shoes, etc. they need.
- She speaks to them with wisdom (not like a fool).
- She instructs and teaches them with kindness.
- She keeps an eye on everything and everyone under her roof; she's watchful and protective.
- She's not idle or lazy; she works hard and her household doesn't suffer from neglect.

4. Has God placed any children (younger brothers, sisters, cousins, children you babysit, etc.) in your life? If so, how can you care for them like an Ideal Woman would?

Answers will vary but may include the following:
- By being willing to help prepare their meals, fix their plates, cut up their food, or feed the baby.
- By helping them with their basic needs (getting dressed; taking baths; brushing teeth, etc.).
- By being an example of kindness and encouragement to them.
- By instructing and helping them learn basic life skills (like picking up their toys, counting, tying their shoes, etc.) and good character (being honest, respectful, sharing with others, etc.).
- By babysitting and gaining experience from caring for children.

5. Think about the time, money, work, etc. involved in taking care of children. Now think about the number of years in her life that a mom spends caring for her kids. With all of that in mind, what specific skills and character qualities will it take for you to care for your future children like the Ideal Woman does?

> Answers will vary but may include the following:
> - Skills: meal-planning, cooking, nutrition, budgeting, the ability to balance job and family responsibilities, the ability to multi-task and delegate, housekeeping skills, organizational skills, etc.
> - Character qualities: spiritual, emotional, and physical strength, wisdom and discernment, a good sense of humor, lots of love and affection, the ability to teach, motivate and instruct, tons of patience, self-discipline, perseverance, energy, and a willingness to work hard for many years.

6. According to Proverbs 31:26-28, how does the Ideal Woman motivate and communicate with her children? How do they feel about her?

> - She uses wise words to communicate to her children – she chooses her words carefully.
> - When she gives them instructions, she does it with kindness – she doesn't bark at them.
> - She motivates them by her own example – she is neither lazy nor neglectful.
> - Her children honor and respect her.

As a mom, I can tell you that receiving a compliment from one of my children means more than almost anything in the world to me. A hug and a kind word from one of my sons can make my spirit soar even on the worst of days. I'm pretty sure your mom feels the very same way.

Girl, have you blessed your mom today? Have you praised or complimented her lately? Let the Lord use you in a HUGE way today. Put your arms around your mom, and say something sweet to her. It'll make you feel good, too.

7. When your future children are grown, what do you want them to remember about you and the kind of mom that you were? What do you hope they'll tell your future grandkids about you?

reflect

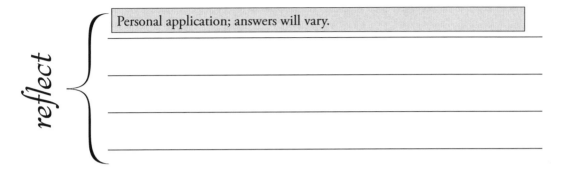

Personal application; answers will vary.

Day Three

pray

1. Wisdom + good sense = a strong house. Today, ask God to give you both wisdom and good sense.

    *A house is built by wisdom and
    becomes strong through good sense.*
    —Proverbs 24:3

Take a look at the very first verse that describes the Ideal Woman:

Who can find a virtuous and capable wife?
—Proverbs 31:10

Notice the first adjective used to describe her. It's the word "virtuous." To some people, this word conjures up a picture of someone who is way too perfect and has absolutely no fun whatsoever. But that's not what "virtuous" means at all. What it actually means is strength, influence, and character.[11]

In Titus 2:4–5, older women are commanded to train younger women to be wise, pure, and to do good to others. The Ideal Woman in Proverbs 31 exemplifies all of these virtues and more. And although you are young, you can possess these virtues, too (I Timothy 4:12).

As you study the Ideal Woman's character today, I want you to "try on" some of the adjectives Proverbs 31 uses to describe her. And trust me—they'll fit. That's one of my favorite things about God's Word. Every verse is one-size-fits-all. Makes "becoming" an Ideal Woman seem very doable!

2. Read and reread Proverbs 31:10–31, and circle the words that describe the Ideal Woman's character and strengths. Also, as you notice specific qualities that you admire about her, record your personal impressions and notes in the margins. Take your time on this. Do not rush.

Proverbs 31:10–31

Notes:

¹³ She's a self-starter.

¹⁴ She shops for bargains.

¹⁶ She invests her money wisely.

¹⁸ She watches the bottom line so she won't waste or lose money.

²¹ She plans and prepare ahead for her family's basic needs.

²² She knows how to sew and decorate.

²² She knows how to dress and takes care of her appearance.

²⁴ She provides extra income for her family.

¹⁰ Who can find a virtuous and capable wife? She is more precious than rubies.

¹¹ Her husband can trust her, and she will greatly enrich his life.

¹² She brings him good, not harm, all the days of her life.

¹³ She finds wool and flax and busily spins it.

¹⁴ She is like a merchant's ship, bringing her food from afar.

¹⁵ She gets up before dawn to prepare breakfast for her household and plan the day's work for her servant girls.

¹⁶ She goes to inspect a field and buys it; with her earnings she plants a vineyard.

¹⁷ She is energetic and strong, a hard worker.

¹⁸ She makes sure her dealings are profitable; her lamp burns late into the night.

¹⁹ Her hands are busy spinning thread, her fingers twisting fiber.

²⁰ She extends a helping hand to the poor and opens her arms to the needy.

²¹ She has no fear of winter for her household, for everyone has warm clothes.

²² She makes her own bedspreads. She dresses in fine linen and purple gowns.

²³ Her husband is well known at the city gates, where he sits with the other civic leaders.

²⁴ She makes belted linen garments and sashes to sell to the merchants.

²⁵ She is clothed with strength and dignity, and she laughs without fear of the future.

²⁶ When she speaks, her words are wise, and she gives instructions with kindness.

²⁷ She carefully watches everything in her household and suffers nothing from laziness.

²⁸ Her children stand and bless her. Her husband praises her:

²⁹ "There are many virtuous and capable women in the world, but you surpass them all!"

³⁰ Charm is deceptive, and beauty does not last; but a woman who fears the Lord will be greatly praised.

³¹ Reward her for all she has done. Let her deeds publicly declare her praise.

3. Record the top three qualities (virtues) you admire about the Ideal Woman.

   # 1 Personal application; answers will vary.

   # 2 _____

   # 3 _____

4. Now, "try on" the top three qualities you selected by completing the following sentences:

   # 1 I can put on this quality by _____

   Personal application; answers will vary.

   # 2 I can put on this quality by _____

   _____

   # 3 I can put on this quality by _____

   _____

5. What would your best friend say are your two best character qualities?

   Personal application; answers will vary.

6. What would you say are your two weakest character qualities, and what can you do to strengthen them?

reflect

   Personal application; answers will vary.

   _____

   _____

   _____

Day Four

pray

1. Before you begin today's lesson, thank God for the wise women He's placed in your life. Ask Him to grow and mature you in wisdom so that you will become a wise woman for others to follow.

> *Wisdom is enshrined in an understanding heart;*
> *wisdom is not found among fools.*
> —Proverbs 14:33

The Ideal Woman is one hard-working gal. It's just one more way that she epitomizes Titus 2:4–5, "Older women must train the younger women…to work in their homes." Although housework may not be the most glamorous thing in the world, our homes and the way we care for them should reflect biblical beauty.

Someday, you'll have your own home to care for, so the first part of today's lesson will focus on the home management skills of the Ideal Woman. Welcome to one of the most down-to-earth, practical parts of our study on biblical beauty: Housework 101.

2. Using the Proverbs 31 passage in yesterday's lesson, compile a list of the responsibilities the Ideal Woman oversees and performs for her home and household.

NOTE: Don't include her business/job responsibilities. We'll study that aspect of her work in a few minutes.

Homekeeping Responsibilities
v. 14 She oversees the shopping and makes sure there are groceries in the house.
v. 15 She oversees the kitchen and meal preparation.
v. 15 She plans and delegates the household chores.
v. 13 / v. 19 / v. 21 } She oversees the clothing needs of her family.
v. 22 She knows how to sew and decorate her home.
v. 27 She is careful and protective of her children, home, and family.

3. How are your homekeeping skills? What can you do today to help around your home and to prepare to keep your own home someday?

> Answers will vary but may include the following:
> *   Help plan the meals and grocery shop.
> *   Learn to cook, sew, decorate, do laundry, iron, and keep house.
> *   Learn to bargain shop.
> *   Participate in the housework and help with daily chores.

You probably noticed that the Ideal Woman had "servant girls" (plural even) to help her. So maybe you're thinking, "When I have a house someday, I'm going to hire a maid or two to help me, too." Hey, if you can afford to hire some help, that's great.

But if you have children in that home you own someday, you need to train them to help and serve around the house (whether you have a maid or not). I used to fuss, mope, and literally seethe at my mother for making me do chores around the house, but now I'm so glad she was unfazed by my pouting. Mother held her ground, made me work, and never let me get by with a second-rate effort—I couldn't "clock out" until I passed her inspection. Because of her strength and fortitude, she managed to teach me (a very unwilling student) how to keep a proper house.

Is housework the Ideal Woman's only work, or does she also work outside the home? And what does God's Word say about wives and moms working outside the home? Find the answers to these questions as you finish today's lesson.

4. Using the Proverbs 31 passage in yesterday's homework, answer the following questions:

    a. Does the Ideal Woman work outside the home? Circle your answer.

        | Yes | No

    b. Record the specific verses from the Proverbs 31 passage that you based your answer upon.

    > Prov. 31:16, 24

5. Earlier this week, you learned how the Ideal Woman takes care of her husband and children. Today you've studied her work inside and outside the home. With everyone she has to take care of and with everything she has to do, how do you think she balances it all? What scriptural evidence do you see in Proverbs 31 about the priorities of the Ideal Woman?

> Answers will vary but may include the following:
> - Her husband is happy and proud of her, so her relationship with him must be a priority.
> - Her children honor and praise her, so her relationship with them is obviously a priority as well.
> - She juggles many responsibilities, but she plans and delegates well.
> - She gets up early, and she's busy (not idle) all day and well into the evening. She manages her time well.
> - Her most important relationship is with God; He is her source of wisdom, strength, and divine balance.

6. How did the Ideal Woman's income impact her family and others? What did you learn about the way she manages her finances?

> Answers will vary but may include the following:
> - She's trustworthy, and that includes the family finances.
> - She makes wise investments that provide extra income and security for her family.
> - She makes sure "her dealings are profitable" which shows she studies, makes informed decisions, and is cautious about her investments.
> - She's generous and giving; she helps the poor and shares with the needy.

7. As you think about your future family, home, and work, what will your priorities be? How will you balance family, home, and career?

reflect

> Personal application; answers will vary.

Day Five

1. For the past six weeks, you've been praying for wisdom using scriptures from the Old Testament Book of Proverbs. But today's scripture is different. It's from the New Testament, and it's a direct quote from the lips of Christ about *wisdom*. A wise young woman's life is a witness to others that God's way—the way of wisdom—is the right way. Praise and thank Him today for the wisdom He's given to you, and ask Him to use your life to point others to Him.

> *But wisdom is shown to be right by the lives of those who follow it.*
> —Luke 7:35

It's our final day of study together. We made it to the finish line! I hope you've enjoyed getting to know the five females from the Proverbs as much as I have. But more than that, I hope you've learned what it takes to become a true beauty—a biblical beauty.

Your study will be light today. I want to give you some extra time to reflect back over the past six weeks and praise the Father for all that He's taught you. Thank you, thank you, precious girl, for your hunger for God's Word and for your commitment to spend time studying it with me. May you enjoy and experience the pleasure of His presence as you meet with Him today.

2. Read Proverbs 31:30–31, and answer the following questions:

   a. The covers of fashion magazines, the experts on infomercials, and the celebs and beauty gurus everywhere all promise the same thing: the secrets of true beauty. They offer potions, programs, and products galore guaranteed to make you beautiful. But what's the real truth about beauty (v. 30)?

   > Physical beauty will fade -- it will not last. It is only temporary.

b. What is the "secret" to biblical beauty (verse 30b)?

> • The fear of the Lord.
> • Reverence for Him.
> • Doing life God's way; obedience.

c. What is the "payoff" for biblical beauty (verses 30b–31)?

> • The praise and respect of others.
> • God's reward upon her life.
> • The results of her life's work; the legacy of a life that made a difference in the lives of others.

3. As your final assignment in this study, take time to praise and thank God for the primary principles He's taught you over the past six weeks. Flip slowly through each lesson in this workbook, and review how He spoke to you through the Immoral Woman, the Indiscreet Woman, the Irritating Woman, the Captivating Woman, and the Ideal Woman. As you review each lesson, complete the following prayer that corresponds with it. Let this be a sweet time of fellowship and overflowing praise to the Lord.

Father, thank you for speaking to me as I studied the Immoral Woman.
I praise and thank you for specifically showing me...

> Personal application; answers will vary.

Father, thank you for speaking to me as I studied the Indiscreet Woman.
 I praise and thank you for specifically showing me...

> Personal application; answers will vary.

Father, thank you for speaking to me as I studied the Irritating Woman.
 I praise and thank you for specifically showing me...

> Personal application; answers will vary.

Father, thank you for speaking to me as I studied the Captivating Woman.
 I praise and thank you for specifically showing me...

> Personal application; answers will vary.

Father, thank you for speaking to me as I studied the Ideal Woman.
 I praise and thank you for specifically showing me...

> Personal application; answers will vary.

At the conclusion of each lesson, I've shared some real-life biblical beauties with you. But just like the Book of Proverbs, I've saved the best for last.

You see, I was raised by an Ideal Woman. Her name is Julia McKay. Virtuous, industrious, energetic and strong, she raised me and my four brothers mostly by herself. I'm sure Mother grew weary as she shouldered the load of raising a large family while Daddy traveled as an evangelist—but she did it. Day by day, she just did it.

And while she did it, she cooked and cleaned, did the laundry and ironed, shopped and kept the pantry filled (an almost impossible task with four boys), oversaw our homework and read to us, got us to church almost every time the doors were open, worked in the yard and gardened, all the while chauffeuring us to piano lessons, football practice, and baseball games.

But it wasn't until I got older that I realized the most important thing Mother had done for us: "She (opened) her mouth in wisdom, and the teaching of kindness (was) on her tongue" (Proverbs 31:26 *NASB*). Somehow in the midst of those crazy, busy days, Mother took snatches of time to teach us eternal truths…and those truths took root and continue to bear fruit.

Mother was not and is not perfect—she'd want you to know that. But she is the most biblically beautiful woman I know. What a privilege to conclude this study by rising up and calling her blessed, and by encouraging you, my precious sister in Christ, to follow in her biblically beautiful footsteps.

P.S. Want to learn more about biblical beauty? Read some of the books on my recommended book list (you'll find it on the following pages). I think you'll love 'em!

Week Six • *Becoming an Ideal Woman*

An Ideal Woman in the making is *becoming:*

1. A *trustworthy*, valuable help to others. *Prov. 31:11–12*

2. A *self-starter* and a hard worker. *Prov. 31:13, 17, 19, 27*

3. A skilled *home keeper* and servant to her family. *Prov. 31:14–15, 21–23*

4. An organized *planner* and overseer. *Prov. 31:15, 21, 27*

5. A wise *investor* and good steward. *Prov. 31:16, 18*

6. A gracious *giver* to those in need. *Prov. 31:20*

7. An excellent *businesswoman*. *Prov. 31:16, 24*

8. A strong, dignified, *confident* woman. *Prov. 31:21, 25*

9. A wise, kind *example*, educator, and encourager. *Prov. 31:26*

   ### *What's her secret? How can she do all this? Answer: Because she is…*

10. A woman who *reverences* God and gives Him priority. *Prov. 31:30*

NOTES:

Week One

[1] contentious. Dictionary.com. *Dictionary.com Unabridged*. Random House, Inc. http://dictionary.reference.com/browse/contentious (accessed: June 02, 2010).

[2] reverence. Dictionary.com. *Dictionary.com Unabridged*. Random House, Inc. http://dictionary.reference.com/browse/reverence (accessed: June 11, 2010).

Week Three

[3] Warren Baker, Eugene Carpenter, *The Complete Word Study Dictionary Old Testament* (Chattanooga, TN: AMG Publishers, 2003), 405.

[4] Ibid.

Week Four

[5] contentious. Dictionary.com. *Dictionary.com Unabridged*. Random House, Inc. http://dictionary.reference.com/browse/contentious (accessed: June 02, 2010).

[6] Spiros Zodhiates, *The Complete Word Study Dictionary New Testament* (Chattanooga, TN: AMG Publishers, 1993), 62.

[7] Ibid, 1031.

[8] Ibid, 1469.

[9] Ibid.

[10] Annie Chapman, *The Mother-in-Law Dance: Can Two Women Love the Same Man and Still Get Along?* (Eugene, Oregon: Harvest House Publishers, 2004), 37.

Week Six

[11] Warren Baker, *The Complete Word Study Dictionary Old Testament* (Chattanooga, TN: AMG Publishers, 2003), 334.

RECOMMENDED BOOKS:

Ruth: A Portrait, The Story of Ruth Bell Graham
By Patricia Cornwell
Doubleday

Teen Virtue 2: A Teen Girl's Guide to Relationships
By Vicki Courtney
Broadman & Holman Publishers

Lies Young Women Believe and the Truth That Sets Them Free
By Nancy Leigh DeMoss
Moody Publishers

For Young Women Only: What You Need to Know About How Guys Think
By Shaunti Feldhahn and Lisa a. Rice
Multnomah Books

A Lineage of Grace
By Francine Rivers
Tyndale House

Big Girls Don't Whine
By Jan Silvious
W Publishing Group

Smart Girls Think Twice
By Jan Silvious
Thomas Nelson

Beauty by The Book *for Teens*

Becoming a Biblically Beautiful Young Woman
A 7-Week Study of Proverbs

Laurie Cole
Author & Teacher

Production Coordinator • Pam Henderson
Cover Design • Debbie Todd
Graphic Design • Julie Riley, j.riley creative LLC
Photography • Don & Mary Carico, Lakewood Photography, League City, TX

Priority Ministries

Encouraging Women to Give God Glory & Priority

www.priorityministries.org

Table of Contents

Course and Discussion *Goals*

GOALS OF Beauty by The Book *for Teens*

The goals of this study are:

1. **To enable** young women to study the Bible and encounter God through the pages of His Word in a life-changing way.

2. **To encourage** young women to become spiritually sensitive and responsive to the work of the Holy Spirit as they apply God's Word to their lives.

3. **To equip** young women to become biblically beautiful.

GOALS FOR CLASS DISCUSSION

Your goal as a class discussion leader is:

1. To facilitate a scripture-based discussion from the daily Bible study homework.

2. To facilitate a Hebrews 10:24 environment where students can share and encourage one another to grow in their relationship with the Lord and to apply His Word to their lives.

"And let us consider how to stimulate
one another to love and good deeds."
—Hebrews 10:24 *NASB*

Basic Information *About This Course*

Beauty by The Book for Teens is a seven-part Bible Study for girls ages 12-19.
To complete the study, each student will need:

1) A *Beauty by The Book for Teens* workbook

2) A Bible or access to an app or online version (www.biblegateway.com)

3) Pencil or pen

4) *Beauty by The Book for Teens* weekly video lecture

5) Optional: access to the web (a few assignments do include online sources; example: p. 30, question 5)

This study contains an introductory video plus six weeks of daily homework assignments which will require approximately 20-25 minutes of classwork per day.

After students complete the daily assignment, you will lead them in a class discussion. **Daily goals, lesson plans, and discussion guides are provided for you on pages 139-173.**

Each week will conclude with a video lecture by Laurie Cole, author of this study. Fill-in-the-blank listening guides are provided in the workbook for students to use during the video. **Completed listening guides are provided for you on pages 1, 21, 43, 61, 83, 107, and 125.**

NOTE: An introductory video lecture should be used on the same day the students start the study.

GRADING & STUDENT ASSESSMENT

Student grades for this study may be based upon one or more of the following:

- Completion of daily/weekly assignments.
- Participation in the daily discussion.
- Weekly Scripture memory.
- Tests (tests are not provided in this guide).

Sample Weekly Lesson Plan

(Daily goals, lesson plans, and discussion guides are provided for you on pages 139-173.)

Monday-Wednesday:

- Students will complete the daily assignment in their workbooks.
- Teacher-led classroom discussion.
- Scripture memory assignment and memory work.

Thursday:

- Scripture memory quiz (ex: have students write out their memory verses).
- Students will complete Day 4 and part of the Day 5 assignment in their workbooks.
- Teacher-led classroom discussion.

NOTE: Depending on how much class time you have, you may need to assign Day 5 as homework.

Friday:

- Students will complete the Day 5 assignment in their workbooks.
- Brief teacher-led classroom discussion.
- Video lecture (approx. 30 minutes); students will take notes using the listening guide provided in their workbooks.

Tips for *Leading an Effective Classroom Discussion*

Daily classroom discussion for *Beauty by The Book for Teens* is vital, and it also should be interesting, inspiring, and enjoyable. The following tips are designed to encourage and enable you to facilitate a positive group discussion:

1. Keep your discussion focused on the two primary goals for class discussion (as stated on page 133).

2. Strive to establish a comfortable, conversational atmosphere so your students will feel free to share what they've studied and learned and what they have on their hearts. Think of your classroom discussion time as a group conversation where everyone has the opportunity to share freely and receive encouragement.

3. As the teacher, facilitate, don't dominate.

4. If a student dominates the discussion, encourage others to participate. You can say, for example, "I'd really like to hear from some of you who haven't shared today."

5. Use the daily discussion guides (provided for you on pages 139-173), but try not to read these questions verbatim or to give students the exact page number corresponding to the question from their workbooks. This will encourage them to restate not repeat (or read) what they've written in their workbooks. They can, of course, use their workbooks to follow along during the discussion, but encourage them not to read their answers verbatim or to limit themselves to sharing only what they've written.

6. Seek to be transparent, genuine, and real in your leadership.

7. Be sensitive to the leadership of the Holy Spirit. If your group gets off track from the discussion guide but you sense the Lord is leading the discussion in a different direction, let Him lead.

8. If you sense a student in your class is hurting or has spiritual questions or needs, you may need to visit with them after class or pray with them. You also may want to encourage them to speak to a school counselor, their parents, a minister, or a Christian counselor.

Daily Lesson Plans
& Discussion Guides

Week One

Monday / Day 1

GOAL:

To introduce students to Proverbs and to the topic of this study: how to become biblically beautiful young women.

LESSON PLAN:

1. Distribute workbooks and Bibles to students.
2. Brief teacher-led classroom discussion (see Discussion Guide below).
3. Introductory video lecture (25:18 minutes); students will complete the fill-in-the-blank listening guide on page 1 in their workbooks.
4. Students complete Week 1, Day 1 assignment. If they are unable to complete it in class, please assign it as homework.
5. Assign weekly memory verse(s). Recommended passage: 1 Samuel 16:7, 1 Peter 3:3-4

DISCUSSION GUIDE:

1. Ask students to turn in their Bibles to Proverbs 1:1-7. Tell them the study they are about to begin is based in Proverbs. Ask someone to read the passage aloud, then ask the following questions:
   - Who wrote Proverbs (v. 1), and why did they write it (vs. 2-4)?
   - In your own words, what is wisdom? What does it mean, and how is it different from knowledge?
   - According to this passage, how do people respond to wisdom (vs. 5, 7b)?
2. Ask students to read Proverbs 1:8-9, then ask the following questions:
   - Who else is Solomon concerned about in this passage (v. 8)? Who needs wisdom, instruction, training, and who is primarily responsible to provide it to them?
   - What characteristics and behaviors does today's culture encourage young women to adopt? Think about what you see on TV, in magazines, in popular music, etc.
   - How does today's culture define beauty, and how does that affect you?
3. Briefly tell your students that this study – *Beauty by The Book for Teens* – will give them the practical wisdom and biblical knowledge they need to become true beauties – biblical beauties – the kind of young women that God will bless and use in an amazing way.
4. Finally, ask them to turn to page 1 in their workbooks and fill in the blanks as they watch the introductory video for this study.

Tuesday / Day 2

GOAL:

To introduce students to the first two females from Proverbs: the Immoral Woman and the Indiscreet Woman.

LESSON PLAN:

1. Students complete Week 1, Day 2 assignment.

   NOTE: As the students work, prepare to lead the discussion by reviewing the Day 1 and Day 2 assignment and answers (pages 2-10).

2. Teacher-led classroom discussion covering Day 1 and Day 2 assignments.

3. Scripture memory work.

DISCUSSION GUIDE:

DAYS ONE & TWO

1. As you studied the Immoral Woman this week, what were your first impressions about her as you read Proverbs 5:3–6? *(ques. 2, p. 3)*

2. As you look at Proverbs 5:3–6, what are some of the characteristics of an Immoral Woman? *(ques. 2, p. 3)*

3. Although your first impression of the Immoral Woman was probably negative, what kind of first impression does she often make with others and why? *(ques. 3a, p. 4)*

4. What kind of reputation does the Immoral Woman have in today's world, and what are some places you most consistently see her? *(ques. 4, p. 4)*

5. Why do you think God reserved five passages and one entire chapter of Proverbs to describe the Immoral Woman? Why do you, a teenage girl, need to know so much about her? *(ques. 5, p. 5)*

6. Who was the second beauty you met in Day 2, and how is she described? *(ques. 2, p. 6)*

7. What is discretion? What does it mean to be "discreet" or "prudent?" *(word search puzzle, p. 7)*

8. What did you learn from Proverbs about Beauty #3, the Irritating Woman? What effect does she have upon others, and how does her behavior impact her relationships? *(ques. 4–5, p. 9)*

9. Can you relate to the Irritating Woman? How and in what relationships? *(ques. 6, p. 10)*

Wednesday / Day 3

GOAL:

To introduce students to the third female from Proverbs: the Irritating Woman.

LESSON PLAN:

1. Students complete Week 1, Day 3 assignment.

   NOTE: As the students work, prepare to lead the discussion by reviewing the Day 3 assignment and answers (pages 11-13).

2. Teacher-led classroom discussion covering Day 3 assignment.

3. Scripture memory work.

DISCUSSION GUIDE:

DAY THREE

1. What did you think when you first read about the Captivating Woman in Proverbs 5:18–19? *(p. 11)* **Note: This is an ice-breaker question—it's not included in their homework—but it will help you segue into discussing this sensual, sexual woman.**

2. According to this passage, who is God encouraging to enjoy sex, and who is the Captivating Woman? *(ques. 3a–c, p. 12)*

3. How does Genesis 2:25 parallel the Captivating Woman passage in Proverbs 5:18–19? *(ques. 5, p. 13)* What do these passages reveal about God's view of sex? What's the difference between the culture's view of sex and God's view of sex? *(ques. 6, p. 13)*

4. As a young, unmarried woman, how did the Lord speak to you as you studied the Captivating Woman? What do you think God is saying to you through her?

Thursday / Day 4

GOAL:

To introduce students to the fourth female from Proverbs: the Captivating Woman.

LESSON PLAN:

1. Scripture memory quiz.
2. Students complete Week 1, Day 4 assignment (and some of Day 5 if possible).
    NOTE: As the students work, prepare to lead the discussion by reviewing the Day 4 assignment and answers (pages 14-16).
3. Teacher-led classroom discussion covering Day 4 assignment.

NOTE: Depending on how much class time you have tomorrow and whether or not you plan to use the Friday video lecture, you may want to assign Day 5 as homework.

DISCUSSION GUIDE:

DAY FOUR

1. What were your first impressions of Beauty #5, the Ideal Woman in Proverbs 31? *(pp. 14–15)*
2. Which qualities, characteristics and accomplishments do you most admire about her and desire for your own life? *(ques. 3, p. 15)*
3. How is the Ideal Woman different from the Immoral Woman? What did you learn about her that reveals she's very different from the Indiscreet Woman? In what way is she different from the Irritating Woman? What does she have in common with the Captivating Woman?
4. How can you prepare today to become an Ideal Woman someday? *(ques. 4, p. 15)*

Friday / Day 5

GOAL:

To introduce students to the fifth female from Proverbs: the Ideal Woman.

LESSON PLAN:

1. Students complete Week 1, Day 5 assignment.

   NOTE: As students work, you may want to take the opportunity to do a cursory check of each student's workbook to see if they completed their daily workbook assignments and to assign their grade. Also, prepare to lead the discussion by reviewing the Day 5 assignment and answers (pages 16-19).

2. Teacher-led classroom discussion covering Day 5 assignment.

3. Week 1 video lecture (27:27 minutes); students use listening guides on page 21 in their workbooks.

DISCUSSION GUIDE:

DAY FIVE

1. What did you learn about biblical beauty from 1 Samuel 16:7 and 1 Peter 3:3–4? How does God define beauty? *(ques. 2a & b, p. 17)*

2. What did you learn about Jesus' physical appearance? *(ques. 3, p. 17)* What do you think attracted people to Jesus?

3. What is your definition of biblical beauty? *(ques. 4, p. 18)*

Week Two

Note: The Day 1 and 2 student assignment and class discussion will include information from the dictionary, the New Living Translation Bible, and several online sources. If students cannot access these sources in the classroom, <u>prior to class, please access and provide this information to them.</u>

These are the sources and information you will need for Monday/Day 1 and Tuesday/Day 2:

- Day 1: The definition of the word "promiscuous" (provided for you on pg. 24, question 2a).

- Day 1: Proverbs 30:20 New Living Translation (provided for you on pg. 25, question 4)

- Day 2: Information to share with your students from the online Modesty Survey at **www.therebelution.com/modestysurvey/browse**. If you have your own computer or laptop available in class, you may want to allow a few girls at a time to study the survey and complete their Day 2 assignment. Or, you may prefer to share information from the survey with them during the class discussion.

- Day 2: *The Modesty Heart Check* is an excellent resource about how to dress modestly. Prior to class, you may want to print a copy for yourself and for your students. You will be using it during the class discussion. To access this resource, visit: **http://girltalk.blogs.com/girltalk/files/modesty_heart_check3.pdf**

Week Two

Monday / Day 1

GOAL:

To understand how the Bible defines and describes immorality and why it is so dangerous.

LESSON PLAN:

1. Students complete Week 2, Day 1 assignment.

   NOTE: If dictionaries are not available, please print the definition for "promiscuous" on the board (see page 24, question 2a). Students will need this definition for today's assignment. Also, as the students work, prepare to lead the discussion by reviewing the Day 1 assignment and answers (pages 22-26).

2. Teacher-led class discussion.

3. Assign weekly memory verse(s). Recommended passages: 1 Timothy 2:9-10, 1 Corinthians 6:19-20

DISCUSSION GUIDE:

DAY ONE

1. You met the Immoral Woman in Proverbs 2:16–19. In this passage, she's also called "promiscuous." Just to make sure we're all clear, what does "promiscuous" mean? *(ques. 2a, p. 24)*

2. What are some of the characteristics of the Immoral Woman? How does she speak? How does she treat God and others? Why is she so dangerous? *(ques. 2b–d & 3, pp. 24–25)*

3. According to Proverbs 30:20, what is her attitude toward her immoral lifestyle? Does she feel any guilt or remorse about her lifestyle or those she hurts? *(ques. 4–5, pp. 25–26)*

4. How did the Lord speak to you through your study today of the Immoral Woman? What insights and wisdom did He give you to protect you from her and her influence?

Tuesday / Day 2

GOAL:

To gain additional wisdom from the Word about the Immoral Woman and to discover God's dress code.

LESSON PLAN:

1. Students complete Week 2, Day 2 assignment.

    NOTE: Please provide students with information from the Modesty Survey or access to the web so they can complete their assignment. Also, as the students work, prepare to lead the discussion by reviewing the Day 2 assignment and answers (pages 27-31).

2. Teacher-led class discussion.

    NOTE: Be sure to have a copy of the Modesty Heart Check to use in the discussion (page 31, question 6 Note - www.girltalk.blogs.com).

3. Scripture memory work.

DISCUSSION GUIDE:

DAY TWO

1. As you examined Proverbs 7:4-27 *(p. 28)*, what else did you notice about the Immoral Woman? What is she like? How does she behave? Share some of the notes and insights you recorded about her. *(ques. 2, pp. 27–28)*

2. Does God care what we wear? What did you learn from 1 Timothy 2:9–10 and 1 Peter 3:3–4 about God's dress code? *(ques. 3, 4b, p. 29)*

3. Discuss the Modesty Survey *(p. 30)*: What about guys? What do they think about modesty and immodesty when it comes to the way girls dress? How does the way a girl dresses affect them? What were some of the most surprising or helpful things you learned about modesty and guys from this survey?

4. Review and discuss the Modesty Heart Check resource. If you printed copies for the girls, pass these out. Enlist 2-3 girls to come to the front of the classroom with you to demonstrate a "top to bottom" modesty check (included in the Modesty Heart Check). Have fun with this.

5. If time allows, ask the girls to share ideas about how to dress in a stylish, fashionable way AND stay within God's dress code. For example, how can they modify today's styles so they are modest and fashionable?

Wednesday / Day 3

GOAL:

To understand the relationship between immoral actions and immoral thoughts, and to discover practical ways to resist temptation.

LESSON PLAN:

1. Students complete Week 2, Day 3 assignment.

   NOTE: As the students work, prepare to lead the discussion by reviewing the Day 3 assignment and answers (pages 31-35).

2. Teacher-led classroom discussion covering Day 3 assignment.

3. Scripture memory work.

DISCUSSION GUIDE:

DAY THREE

1. Where does immorality begin? What did you learn from Mark 7:21–23? *(ques. 2a, p. 32)*

2. Is immorality always a physical act? What does Jesus teach about immorality in Matthew 5:27–28? *(ques. 3a, p. 33)*

3. Is the following statement true or false: "Just because you're a Christian doesn't mean you can't be sexy. And if a guy is tempted because you're dressed hot, that's his problem. He shouldn't be looking."? *(ques. 4, p. 33)*

4. What are some ways we can resist sexual temptation:
   - in our thought life?
   - when we're watching television?
   - when we're surfing the internet or online?
   - when we're reading magazines or books?
   - when we're watching movies?
   - when guys flirt, speak, or behave in a sexually suggestive way?
   - when conversations with other girls become sexually suggestive or explicit? *(ques. 5, p. 34)*

Thursday / Day 4

GOAL:

To understand why sexual purity is so important to God.

LESSON PLAN:

1. Scripture memory quiz.
2. Students complete Week 2, Day 4 assignment (and some of Day 5 if possible).

    NOTE: As the students work, prepare to lead the discussion by reviewing the Day 4 assignment and answers (pages 35-38).
3. Teacher-led classroom discussion.

NOTE: Depending on how much class time you have tomorrow and whether or not you plan to use the Friday video lecture, you may want to assign Day 5 as homework.

DISCUSSION GUIDE:

DAY FOUR

1. What did you learn from 1 Corinthians 6:12–20 about immorality and the Christian? Why is sexual purity so important to God? *(ques. 2 & 3a–e, pp. 36–37)*
2. According to 1 Thessalonians 4:3–7, what is God's will and sexual standard for you, His daughter? *(ques. 4a, p. 37)* How can you keep yourself pure? *(ques. 4b, p. 37)*
3. Are there consequences for sexual immorality? What did you learn from 1 Thessalonians 4 and Hebrews 13? *(ques. 4c & 5, pp. 37–38)*
4. If a friend told you that she was considering having sex with her boyfriend, what would you tell her? How could you effectively share some of the things you've studied today with her?

Friday / Day 5

GOAL:

To understand God's grace and forgiveness for sin – even immorality.

LESSON PLAN:

1. Students complete Week 2, Day 5 assignment.

   NOTE: As students work, you may want to take the opportunity to do a cursory check of each student's workbook to see if they completed their daily workbook assignments and to assign their grade. Also, prepare to lead the discussion by reviewing the Day 5 assignment and answers (pages 38-42).

2. Teacher-led classroom discussion covering Day 5 assignment.

3. Week 2 video lecture (27:26 minutes); students use listening guides on page 43 in their workbooks.

DISCUSSION GUIDE:

DAY FIVE

1. Can God forgive immorality? What did you learn as you studied the genealogy of Jesus in Matthew 1? *(ques. 2, p. 39)* What does this reveal about God?

2. How did Jesus deal with the woman caught in adultery, and what does His example teach us? *(ques. 4b–c, p 41)*

3. If a friend told you that she'd had sex with a guy and that she now she regretted it and was ashamed and embarrassed about it, what would you tell her? How would you encourage and minister to her?

4. What's the most important thing you learned this week that will help you become a more biblically beautiful young woman?

5. Close your small group time by affirming your group of God's love for each one of them. Let them know that if they have doubts about their salvation, or are dealing with guilt from past sins or immorality, you are available and would love to visit with them after small group.

Week Three

Monday / Day 1

GOAL:

To understand the necessity and characteristics of discretion.

LESSON PLAN:

1. Students complete Week 3, Day 1 assignment.

   NOTE: As the students work, prepare to lead the discussion by reviewing the Day 1 assignment and answers (pages 44-47).

2. Teacher-led class discussion.

3. Assign weekly memory verse(s). Recommended passages: Proverbs 3:21-25

DISCUSSION GUIDE:

DAY ONE

1. What is discretion? What is indiscretion, and why is it so dangerous? *(ques. 2, p. 46)*

2. According to Proverbs 3:21–26, what are the benefits of discretion? *(ques. 3, p. 46)*

3. Discretion and prudence are very much alike, and indiscretion and foolishness go hand-in-hand. What are some of the differences between a discreet/prudent person and a foolish/indiscreet person? *(chart on page 47)*

4. How did the scriptures you studied from Proverbs about discretion and prudence speak to you? What practical insights did you gain from them to apply to your life and relationships with others? *(ques. 5, p. 47)*

Tuesday / Day 2

GOAL:

To know Abigail, a role model of wisdom and discretion.

LESSON PLAN:

1. Students complete Week 3, Day 2 assignment.

    NOTE: While your students work, prepare for today's discussion by reading 1 Samuel 25:1-42 (pages 176-177), the story of Abigail and reviewing the Day 2 assignment and answers (pages 48-50).

2. Teacher-led class discussion.

3. Scripture memory work.

DISCUSSION GUIDE:

DAY TWO

1. Who was Abigail, and what was she like? What was her husband like? *(ques. 2a–b, pp. 48–49)*

2. What was going on in Abigail's life and home when you read about her in 1 Samuel 25? What choice did she make when her servant informed her of Nabal's decision? *(ques. 2c, p. 49)* If she had chosen to ignore discretion and do nothing, what could have happened? How did Abigail's speech and decisions reveal her discretion and wisdom? *(ques. 2d, p. 49)*

3. What immediate and future benefits did Abigail receive because of her discretion and prudence? *(ques. 2e & g, pp. 49–50)*

4. Why is Abigail a role model of discretion and wisdom? Do you know any real-life "Abigails" – wise women you respect and admire? Share who they are, and describe what they have in common with Abigail.

5. What insights did you learn from Abigail to help you deal with the foolish people in your life? *(ques. 3, p. 50)*

Wednesday / Day 3

GOAL:

To understand the characteristics and results of discretion and that it is available to those who are young.

LESSON PLAN:

1. Students complete Week 3, Day 3 assignment.

    NOTE: While your students work, prepare for today's discussion by reading 1 Samuel 16:14-22 and Genesis 41:38-44 (see page 178), the stories of David and Joseph, and reviewing the Day 3 assignment and answers (pages 50-52).

2. Teacher-led classroom discussion.

3. Scripture memory work.

DISCUSSION GUIDE:

DAY THREE

1. What kind of young man was David? What did you learn about his character in 1 Samuel 16? *(ques. 2a, p. 51)*

2. You also studied Joseph, another young man whose life was marked by wisdom, discretion, and discernment. What was the result of Joseph's discretion? How did God use him? *(ques. 3a–b, pp. 51–52)*

3. Both David and Joseph displayed wisdom, discretion and discernment at a young age. What does this reveal about discretion, wisdom, and discernment? *(ques. 4, p. 52)*

4. As a young woman, how can you display these same characteristics? What did you learn from Proverbs 20:11? *(ques. 4, p. 52)*

5. What about you? How are you doing when it comes to discretion? *(ques. 5, p. 52)*

Thursday / Day 4

GOAL:

To understand why discretion is so important in friendships and indiscretion is so dangerous to them.

LESSON PLAN:

1. Scripture memory quiz.
2. Students complete Week 3, Day 4 assignment (and some of Day 5 if possible).

   NOTE: While your students work, prepare for today's discussion by reading Daniel 2:12-19, 24-28 (see page 179), the story of Daniel and reviewing the Day 4 assignment and answers (pages 53-55).
3. Teacher-led classroom discussion.

NOTE: Depending on how much class time you have tomorrow and whether or not you plan to use the Friday video lecture, you may want to assign Day 5 as homework.

DISCUSSION GUIDE:

DAY FOUR

1. What kind of guy was Daniel? How was he described in Daniel 2:12–19? *(ques. 2a, p. 53)*
2. What was the result of Daniel's wisdom, discretion, and prudence? *(ques. 2b, p. 53)*
3. Abigail, Joseph, David, and Daniel all possessed discretion, wisdom, and discernment as well as a common faith in God. But what other common ties did you see in their lives and stories? *(ques. 3, p. 54)* **LEADER NOTE: They were all promoted/rewarded for their discretion. Not only is discretion and wisdom often rewarded, these characteristics are also often recognized by people in positions of authority. Joseph, David, and Daniel were also all young which reveals that discretion has no age limitations. Lastly, the discretion God gave them saved and benefited the lives of countless others.**
4. Friendship is so important. What did you learn from Proverbs that will help you preserve your friendships with others? *(ques. 4a–e, pp. 54–55)*
5. How and with whom are you most challenged to be discreet? What practical things can you do to become a woman of discretion? *(ques. 6, p. 55)*

Friday / Day 5

GOAL:

To discover that wisdom is available from God to all who will seek and obey Him and study His Word.

LESSON PLAN:

1. Students complete Week 3, Day 5 assignment.

   NOTE: As students work, you may want to take the opportunity to do a cursory check of each student's workbook to see if they completed their daily workbook assignments and to assign their grade. Also, prepare to lead the discussion by reviewing the Day 5 assignment and answers (pages 56-59).

2. Teacher-led classroom discussion covering Day 5 assignment.

3. Week 3 video lecture (26.39 minutes); students use listening guides on page 61 in their workbooks.

DISCUSSION GUIDE:

DAY FIVE

1. How can you get wisdom? What did you learn from James 1:5-8? *(ques. 2a–e, p. 57)*

2. How can you grow in wisdom? What did you learn from Psalm 119, Proverbs 13, and 1 Peter 2? *(ques. 3a–c, pp. 57–58)*

3. In what areas of your life and relationships do you need a good dose of discretion?

Week Four

Monday / Day 1

GOAL:

To understand the characteristics and dangers of becoming an Irritating Woman.

LESSON PLAN:

1. Students complete Week 4, Day 1 assignment.

   NOTE: While your students work, prepare for today's discussion by reading 2 Samuel 6:16-23 (see page 180), the story of David and Michal, and reviewing the Day 1 assignment and answers (pages 62-66).

2. Teacher-led class discussion.

3. Assign weekly memory verse(s). Recommended passages: Proverbs 21:9 & 19, Ephesians 4:29

DISCUSSION GUIDE:

DAY ONE

1. What adjectives does Proverbs use to describe the Irritating Woman? *(ques. 2a, p. 64)* What do *you* call a woman like this? *(ques. 2b, p. 64)*

2. What effect does the Irritating Woman have upon others? How does she make them feel? *(ques. 2c, p. 65)* Imagine that you're sitting at the school lunch table with a group of girls, and one of them is an Irritating Young Woman. Without naming names (remember your lesson on discretion last week ☺), what impact can that one Irritating Young Woman have upon the entire group?

3. Does the Irritating Woman's behavior cost her anything? What did you learn from Proverbs? *(ques. 2d, p. 65)*

4. What did you learn from your study of Michal (David's wife)? What insights did you learn from her about the heart, mind, and behavior of the Irritating Woman? *(ques. 3a–d, pp. 65–66)* What did her irritating, contentious behavior cost her? *(ques. 3e, p. 66)*

Tuesday / Day 2

GOAL:

To understand the root cause of the Irritating Woman's behavior.

LESSON PLAN:

1. Students complete Week 4, Day 2 assignment.

   NOTE: While your students work, prepare for today's discussion by reading Numbers 12:1-15 (see page 181), the story of Miriam and Moses, and reviewing the Day 2 assignment and answers (pages 67-71).

2. Teacher-led class discussion.

3. Scripture memory work.

DISCUSSION GUIDE:

DAY TWO

1. Ask your group to raise their hand if, at times, they struggle with becoming an Irritating Young Woman. Next, ask them why all women struggle with the desire to nag, complain, and control. *(ques. 2a, p. 68, and notes on pp. 68–69)*

2. What did you learn about Miriam from Exodus 15:19-21? What caused her to go into Irritating Woman mode? *(ques. 3a, pp. 69–70)* What do you think was at the root of Miriam's problem with her brother, Moses, and what do you think she sought to gain by her behavior? *(ques. 3b–c, p. 70)* Did Miriam get what she wanted? What were the consequences of her behavior, and what can we learn from this? *(ques. 3d, p. 70)*

3. What about you? Has anything or anyone set off the Irritating Woman in you lately? How? *(ques. 4, p. 70)*

4. As you listed the authority figures God has placed in your life, which ones do you most feel the need to nag, complain, control and argue with? *(ques. 5, p. 71)*

Wednesday / Day 3

GOAL:

To learn the right way to handle problems without becoming an Irritating Woman.

LESSON PLAN:

1. Students complete Week 4, Day 3 assignment.

   NOTE: While your students work, prepare for today's discussion by reading Numbers 27:1-11, 36:1-12 (see pages 182-183), the story of the daughters of Zelophehad, and reviewing the Day 3 assignment and answers (pages 72-74).

2. Teacher-led classroom discussion.

3. Scripture memory work.

DISCUSSION GUIDE:

DAY THREE

1. This week you studied very cool group of sisters: the daughters of Zelophehad. What problems and dire circumstances did they face? How did they handle it? What characteristics did they display through their dealings with those in authority over them? *(top half of chart, p. 73)*

2. How would an Irritating Woman likely handle a problem like theirs, and what possible negative fallout could occur? What immediate and long-term benefits occurred as a result of the way the daughters of Zelophehad handled their problem? *(lower half of chart, p. 73)*

3. What unjust circumstances or problems have you ever experienced? How did the example of the daughters of Zelophehad encourage you to respond to injustice? *(ques. 3, p. 74)*

Thursday / Day 4

GOAL:

To discover how to speak fluent 3B (words that build, bless, and benefit).

LESSON PLAN:

1. Scripture memory quiz.
2. Students complete Week 4, Day 4 assignment.

   NOTE: While your students work, prepare for today's discussion by reviewing the Day 4 assignment and answers (pages 74-77).
3. Teacher-led classroom discussion.

NOTE: Depending on how much class time you have tomorrow and whether or not you plan to use the Friday video lecture, you may want to assign Day 5 as homework.

DISCUSSION GUIDE:

DAY FOUR

1. What is the cure for 3C behavior and speech? According to Ephesians 4:29, what are the only kinds of words we're allowed to speak? *(ques. 3, pp. 75–76)*
2. According to Proverbs, what do 3B words look and sound like? What can 3B words do for those who hear and speak them? *(ques. 4, p. 76)*

Friday / Day 5

GOAL:

To discover more about how to speak fluent 3B.

LESSON PLAN:

1. Students complete Week 4, Day 5 assignment.

   NOTE: As students work, you may want to take the opportunity to do a cursory check of each student's workbook to see if they completed their daily workbook assignments and to assign their grade. Also, prepare to lead the discussion by reviewing the Day 5 assignment and answers (pages 77-81).

2. Teacher-led classroom discussion covering Day 5 assignment.

3. Week 4 video lecture (29:54 minutes); students use listening guides on page 83 in their workbooks.

DISCUSSION GUIDE:

DAY FIVE

1. What did you learn about biblically beautiful speech and behavior from 1 Peter 3:1–4? *(ques. 2, p. 78)*

2. What about cussing? What did you learn from James 3:6-12 about the power of the tongue and the words you speak? *(ques. 3, p. 79)*

3. What tips for talking did you pick up from Proverbs? *(ques. 4, p. 80)*

Week Five

Monday / Day 1

GOAL:

To discover the faith and character of a captivating young woman.

LESSON PLAN:

1. Students complete Week 5, Day 1 assignment.

    NOTE: While your students work, prepare for today's discussion by reviewing the Day 1 assignment and answers (pages 84-88).

2. Teacher-led class discussion.

3. Assign weekly memory verse(s). Recommended passages: Ruth 1:16-17, 2 Corinthians 6:14

DISCUSSION GUIDE:

DAY ONE

1. Read Proverbs 5:18–19 aloud to your group *(ques. 2, p. 86)*. Tell your group that this passage describes the Captivating Woman, an amazing biblical beauty. Ask your group, "What kind of woman is this? Who is the Captivating Woman?" *(answers: a fountain of blessing to her husband; a wife; a married woman; a wife whose love and sexuality captivates and satisfies her husband.)*

2. Ask your group, "What does this sensuous passage reveal about how God views sex? *(answers: He views sex as a beautiful form of love between a husband and wife; He blesses sex within marriage; He says that it is something a husband and wife should rejoice in and enjoy; He encourages husbands and wives to enjoy a satisfying, sexual relationship.)* What does this passage teach you about the kind of wife you should be someday?

3. Take time to encourage your group to become a Captivating Woman someday should they marry. But also encourage them to remain sexually pure until marriage so they can experience God's best for them when they do marry. Although the culture may encourage them to become sexually active "when they're ready," or "when they're in a committed relationship with someone special," God reserves sex—the most intimate, sacred act between a man and a woman—for marriage.

4. Tell your group that although they cannot be Captivating Women— sensual, sexual women—until they get married, they can be Captivating Young Women, the kind of girls that guys find fascinating and attractive. This week they studied someone just like that: Ruth. What did you learn about Ruth in Ruth Chapter 1? *(cover ques. 4a–e, pp. 87–88)*

5. What qualities did Ruth possess that would make her a great friend? *(ques. 5, p. 88)*

Tuesday / Day 2

GOAL:

To understand how Ruth handled herself around others (including Boaz), the characteristics that made her attractive, and the character traits of Boaz.

LESSON PLAN:

1. Students complete Week 5, Day 2 assignment.

   NOTE: While your students work, prepare for today's discussion by reviewing the Day 2 assignment and answers (pages 89-93).

2. Teacher-led class discussion.

3. Scripture memory work.

DISCUSSION GUIDE:

DAY TWO

1. How did Ruth meet Boaz? What did you learn from Ruth Chapter 2? *(ques. 3a–e, pp. 90–91)*

2. What kind of guy was Boaz? *(ques. 3f, p. 92)* What characteristics did you admire and respect about him? In what ways is he like the kind of guy you'd like to date or marry someday? *(ques. 4, p. 93)*

Wednesday / Day 3

GOAL:

To discover how to know if a guy really loves you.

LESSON PLAN:

1. Students complete Week 5, Day 3 assignment.

   NOTE: While your students work, prepare for today's discussion by reading the Day 3 assignment and answers (pages 93-96).

2. Teacher-led classroom discussion.

3. Scripture memory work.

DISCUSSION GUIDE:

DAY THREE

1. How did Ruth and Boaz ever get together? Since they didn't really date back them, what happened that eventually led to their commitment to one another? What did you learn from Ruth Chapter 3? *(ques. 3a, p. 95)*

2. Put yourself in Ruth's shoes. If Naomi had told you to go to the threshing floor, wait for Boaz to fall asleep, then lay at his feet, what would you have done? *(ques. 3c, p. 95)* Ruth did exactly what Naomi told her. What does this reveal about Ruth? ***(answer: She trusted Naomi's counsel, wisdom, and she trusted God; she was also courageous in seeking a commitment from Boaz; he could have rejected her.)***

3. Read Boaz's response (Ruth 3:10–15) to Ruth to your group *(pp. 94–95)*

4. What commitment did Boaz make to Ruth? How did he prove that he was sincere in his commitment? *(ques. 4, p. 96)*

5. Based on what you learned from Boaz, how can you tell whether or not a guy is really sincere in his love and commitment to you? ***(ques. 5, p. 96; answer: he will protect you and your purity; he won't pressure or use you; he will provide for your needs; he will follow through with his commitment.)***

Thursday / Day 4

GOAL:

To discover how Boaz demonstrated his love and commitment to Ruth.

LESSON PLAN:

1. Scripture memory quiz.
2. Students complete Week 5, Day 4 assignment.

   NOTE: While your students work, prepare for today's discussion by reviewing the Day 4 assignment and answers (pages 97-100).

3. Teacher-led classroom discussion.

NOTE: Depending on how much class time you have tomorrow and whether or not you plan to use the Friday video lecture, you may want to assign Day 5 as homework.

DISCUSSION GUIDE:

DAY FOUR

1. Ruth Chapter 4 reveals the beautiful ending of the story of Ruth and Boaz. How did their story end? How did Boaz prove his commitment to Ruth? *(ques. 3a, p. 98)* How do you think Ruth felt when she heard about the way Boaz had publicly proclaimed his desire to marry her? *(ques. 3b, p. 99)*

2. How did God bless Ruth and Boaz? *(ques. 3c, p. 99)*

   What did you learn about the importance of making good choices even when it's hard? *(ques. 4a, p. 99)*

3. What did you learn about the importance of making good choices even when it's hard? *(ques. 4a, p. 99)*

4. Why do you think God recorded this love story between Ruth and Boaz in the Bible? *(ques. 4b, p. 99)*

5. What characteristics in Ruth's life do you most desire in yours? *(ques. 5, p. 100)*

Friday / Day 5

GOAL:

To discover God's #1 requirement for any guy we date or marry, and how to know if they meet that requirement.

LESSON PLAN:

1. Students complete Week 5, Day 5 assignment.

   NOTE: As students work, you may want to take the opportunity to do a cursory check of each student's workbook to see if they completed their daily workbook assignments and to assign their grade. Also, prepare to lead the discussion by reviewing the Day 5 assignment and answers (pages 100-105).

2. Teacher-led classroom discussion covering Day 5 assignment.

3. Week 5 video lecture (32:10 minutes); students use listening guides on page 107 in their workbooks.

DISCUSSION GUIDE:

DAY FIVE

1. What did you learn from Ruth about how to attract a godly guy? Why do you think Boaz was attracted to her? Why do you think Ruth was attracted to Boaz? *(ques. 2, chart p. 101)*

2. What is God's #1 requirement for any guy that you date? *(ques. 3, p. 102)*

   How can you know if a guy meets this requirement? What should you look for? What did you learn from Matthew 7 and Galatians 5? *(ques. 4a–b, p. 103)*

3. What kind of guy do you want to say, "I do," to? *(ques. 5, p. 104)*

4. What characteristics in Ruth's life do you most desire in yours? *(ques. 5, p. 100)*

Week Six

Monday / Day 1

GOAL:

To discover how to demonstrate love to your future husband.

LESSON PLAN:

1. Students complete Week 6, Day 1 assignment.

    NOTE: While your students work, prepare for today's discussion by reviewing the Day 1 assignment and answers (pages 108-112).

2. Teacher-led class discussion.

3. Assign weekly memory verse(s). Recommended passages: Proverbs 31:10-12, 28-31

DISCUSSION GUIDE:

DAY ONE

1. Who is the Ideal Woman's biggest fan? What did you learn about her relationship with her husband? *(ques. 2, scriptures, p.110)*

2. Why is trust essential for a strong relationship? *(ques. 3a, p. 110)* Why is trust especially important between a husband and wife? *(ques. 3b, p. 111)* If you marry someday, how can you earn your husband's trust? *(ques. 3c, p. 111)* Okay, so what can you do *today* to become the kind of wife your future husband will trust? *(ques. 3d, p. 111)*

3. The Ideal Woman helps and enriches her husband's life (verses 10–12). What are some practical ways a wife can help her husband succeed and excel? *(ques. 4, p. 111)*

4. Proverbs 31 never says that the Ideal Woman loves her husband, but how do you know that she did? *(ques. 5, p. 112)*

Tuesday / Day 2

GOAL:

To discover how to demonstrate love to your future children.

LESSON PLAN:

1. Students complete Week 6, Day 2 assignment.

   NOTE: While your students work, prepare for today's discussion by reviewing the Day 2 assignment and answers (pages 112-115).

2. Teacher-led class discussion.

3. Scripture memory work.

DISCUSSION GUIDE:

DAY TWO

1. What are some of the specific ways the Ideal Woman takes care of her children? *(ques. 3, p. 113)*

2. Has the Lord placed any children in your life? Share some of the opportunities you've had to care for children and be (kind of) the "mom." *(ques. 4, p. 113)* What are some of the challenges involved in caring for children? What specific skills and qualities will it take for you to care for your future children like the Ideal Woman does? *(ques. 5, p. 114)*

3. How does the Ideal Woman communicate and motivate her children? How do they feel about her? *(ques. 6, p. 114)*

4. How many of you hugged your mom this week and said something sweet to her? How did she respond?

5. What kind of mom do you want to be someday? What do you want your kids to tell your grandkids about you? *(ques. 7, p. 115)*

Wednesday / Day 3

GOAL:

To discover how to practice and apply the qualities of the Ideal Woman as a young woman.

LESSON PLAN:

1. Students complete Week 6, Day 3 assignment.

   NOTE: While your students work, prepare for today's discussion by reviewing the Day 3 assignment and answers (pages 115-117).

2. Teacher-led classroom discussion.

3. Scripture memory work.

DISCUSSION GUIDE:

DAY THREE

1. As you read and reread Proverbs 31, what other character qualities did you notice about the Ideal Woman? What are some of the words that you circled? *(ques. 2, p. 116)*

2. What are the top three qualities that you admire about the Ideal Woman? *(ques. 3, p. 117)*

3. What would your best friend say are your two best character qualities? *(ques. 5, p. 117)*. What are a couple of your weakest character qualities, and how can you strengthen them? *(ques. 6, 117)*

Thursday / Day 4

GOAL:

To discover the work ethic and habits of the Ideal Woman.

LESSON PLAN:

1. Scripture memory quiz.
2. Students complete Week 6, Day 4 assignment.

   NOTE: While your students work, prepare for today's discussion by reviewing the Day 4 assignment and answers (pages 118-120).

3. Teacher-led classroom discussion.

NOTE: Depending on how much class time you have tomorrow and whether or not you plan to use the Friday video lecture, you may want to assign Day 5 as homework.

DISCUSSION GUIDE:

DAY FOUR

1. How does the Ideal Woman care for her home? What homekeeping responsibilities does she oversee and perform? *(ques. 2, p.118)* What are you doing today to help around your home? What homekeeping skills do you need to learn and practice in order to take care of your own home someday? *(ques. 3, p. 119)*
2. Does the Ideal Woman work outside the home? What scriptural evidence did you see? *(ques. 4a–b, p. 119)*
3. The Ideal Woman has her hands full! How does she do all that she does? What scriptural evidence did you see in Proverbs 31 about her priorities? *(ques. 5, p. 120)*

Friday / Day 5

GOAL:

To discover the secret of biblical beauty; to review what students have learned from all five females from Proverbs.

LESSON PLAN:

1. Students complete Week 6, Day 5 assignment.

    NOTE: As students work, you may want to take the opportunity to do a cursory check of each student's workbook to see if they completed their daily workbook assignments and to assign their grade. Also, prepare to lead the discussion by reviewing the Day 5 assignment and answers (pages 121-124).

2. Teacher-led classroom discussion covering Day 5 assignment.
3. Week 6 video lecture (34:05 minutes); students use listening guides on page 125 in their workbooks.

DISCUSSION GUIDE:

DAY FIVE

1. What's the real truth about physical beauty? What happens to it? *(ques. 2a, p. 121)*
2. What is the "secret" to biblical beauty/true beauty? *(ques. 2b, p. 122)* What is the reward—the payoff—for biblical beauty? *(ques. 2c, p. 122)*
3. What's the biggest thing God has taught you as you've studied His Word for the past six weeks? What's the most important thing that He's done in your life as He's taught you about biblical beauty?
4. Conclude your final day of this study by praying aloud for your students. Ask God to continue to grow each one of them into biblically beautiful young women of God.

Bible Scripture
References

Week Three, Day 2

Question 2 (p. 48)

1 Samuel 25:1-42 *(NLT)*

[1] Now Samuel died, and all Israel gathered for his funeral. They buried him at his house in Ramah.

Then David moved down to the wilderness of Maon. [2] There was a wealthy man from Maon who owned property near the town of Carmel. He had 3,000 sheep and 1,000 goats, and it was sheep-shearing time. [3] This man's name was Nabal, and his wife, Abigail, was a sensible and beautiful woman. But Nabal, a descendant of Caleb, was crude and mean in all his dealings.

[4] When David heard that Nabal was shearing his sheep, [5] he sent ten of his young men to Carmel with this message for Nabal: [6] "Peace and prosperity to you, your family, and everything you own! [7] I am told that it is sheep-shearing time. While your shepherds stayed among us near Carmel, we never harmed them, and nothing was ever stolen from them. [8] Ask your own men, and they will tell you this is true. So would you be kind to us, since we have come at a time of celebration? Please share any provisions you might have on hand with us and with your friend David." [9] David's young men gave this message to Nabal in David's name, and they waited for a reply.

[10] "Who is this fellow David?" Nabal sneered to the young men. "Who does this son of Jesse think he is? There are lots of servants these days who run away from their masters. [11] Should I take my bread and my water and my meat that I've slaughtered for my shearers and give it to a band of outlaws who come from who knows where?"

[12] So David's young men returned and told him what Nabal had said. [13] "Get your swords!" was David's reply as he strapped on his own. Then 400 men started off with David, and 200 remained behind to guard their equipment.

[14] Meanwhile, one of Nabal's servants went to Abigail and told her, "David sent messengers from the wilderness to greet our master, but he screamed insults at them. [15] These men have been very good to us, and we never suffered any harm from them. Nothing was stolen from us the whole time they were with us. [16] In fact, day and night they were like a wall of protection to us and the sheep. [17] You need to know this and figure out what to do, for there is going to be trouble for our master and his whole family. He's so ill-tempered that no one can even talk to him!"

[18] Abigail wasted no time. She quickly gathered 200 loaves of bread, two wineskins full of wine, five sheep that had been slaughtered, nearly a bushel of roasted grain, 100 clusters of raisins, and 200 fig cakes. She packed them on donkeys [19] and said to her servants, "Go on ahead. I will follow you shortly." But she didn't tell her husband Nabal what she was doing.

[20] As she was riding her donkey into a mountain ravine, she saw David and his men coming toward her. [21] David had just been saying, "A lot of good it did to help this fellow. We protected his flocks in the wilderness, and nothing he owned was lost or stolen. But he has repaid me evil for good. [22] May God strike me and kill me if even one man of his household is still alive tomorrow morning!"

²³ When Abigail saw David, she quickly got off her donkey and bowed low before him. ²⁴ She fell at his feet and said, "I accept all blame in this matter, my lord. Please listen to what I have to say. ²⁵ I know Nabal is a wicked and ill-tempered man; please don't pay any attention to him. He is a fool, just as his name suggests. But I never even saw the young men you sent.

²⁶ "Now, my lord, as surely as the Lord lives and you yourself live, since the Lord has kept you from murdering and taking vengeance into your own hands, let all your enemies and those who try to harm you be as cursed as Nabal is. ²⁷ And here is a present that I, your servant, have brought to you and your young men. ²⁸ Please forgive me if I have offended you in any way. The Lord will surely reward you with a lasting dynasty, for you are fighting the Lord's battles. And you have not done wrong throughout your entire life.

²⁹ "Even when you are chased by those who seek to kill you, your life is safe in the care of the Lord your God, secure in his treasure pouch! But the lives of your enemies will disappear like stones shot from a sling! ³⁰ When the Lord has done all he promised and has made you leader of Israel, ³¹ don't let this be a blemish on your record. Then your conscience won't have to bear the staggering burden of needless bloodshed and vengeance. And when the Lord has done these great things for you, please remember me, your servant!"

³² David replied to Abigail, "Praise the Lord, the God of Israel, who has sent you to meet me today! ³³ Thank God for your good sense! Bless you for keeping me from murder and from carrying out vengeance with my own hands. ³⁴ For I swear by the Lord, the God of Israel, who has kept me from hurting you, that if you had not hurried out to meet me, not one of Nabal's men would still be alive tomorrow morning." ³⁵ Then David accepted her present and told her, "Return home in peace. I have heard what you said. We will not kill your husband."

³⁶ When Abigail arrived home, she found that Nabal was throwing a big party and was celebrating like a king. He was very drunk, so she didn't tell him anything about her meeting with David until dawn the next day. ³⁷ In the morning when Nabal was sober, his wife told him what had happened. As a result he had a stroke, and he lay paralyzed on his bed like a stone. ³⁸ About ten days later, the Lord struck him, and he died.

³⁹ When David heard that Nabal was dead, he said, "Praise the Lord, who has avenged the insult I received from Nabal and has kept me from doing it myself. Nabal has received the punishment for his sin." Then David sent messengers to Abigail to ask her to become his wife.

⁴⁰ When the messengers arrived at Carmel, they told Abigail, "David has sent us to take you back to marry him."

⁴¹ She bowed low to the ground and responded, "I, your servant, would be happy to marry David. I would even be willing to become a slave, washing the feet of his servants!" ⁴² Quickly getting ready, she took along five of her servant girls as attendants, mounted her donkey, and went with David's messengers. And so she became his wife.

Week Three, Day 3

Question 2 (p. 51)

1 Samuel 16:14-22 *(NLT)*

14 Now the Spirit of the Lord had left Saul, and the Lord sent a tormenting spirit that filled him with depression and fear.

15 Some of Saul's servants said to him, "A tormenting spirit from God is troubling you. 16 Let us find a good musician to play the harp whenever the tormenting spirit troubles you. He will play soothing music, and you will soon be well again."

17 "All right," Saul said. "Find me someone who plays well, and bring him here."

18 One of the servants said to Saul, "One of Jesse's sons from Bethlehem is a talented harp player. Not only that—he is a brave warrior, a man of war, and has good judgment. He is also a fine-looking young man, and the Lord is with him."

19 So Saul sent messengers to Jesse to say, "Send me your son David, the shepherd." 20 Jesse responded by sending David to Saul, along with a young goat, a donkey loaded with bread, and a wineskin full of wine.

21 So David went to Saul and began serving him. Saul loved David very much, and David became his armor bearer.

22 Then Saul sent word to Jesse asking, "Please let David remain in my service, for I am very pleased with him."

Question 3 (p. 51)

Genesis 41:38-44 *(NLT)*

38 So Pharaoh asked his officials, "Can we find anyone else like this man so obviously filled with the spirit of God?" 39 Then Pharaoh said to Joseph, "Since God has revealed the meaning of the dreams to you, clearly no one else is as intelligent or wise as you are. 40 You will be in charge of my court, and all my people will take orders from you. Only I, sitting on my throne, will have a rank higher than yours."

41 Pharaoh said to Joseph, "I hereby put you in charge of the entire land of Egypt." 42 Then Pharaoh removed his signet ring from his hand and placed it on Joseph's finger. He dressed him in fine linen clothing and hung a gold chain around his neck. 43 Then he had Joseph ride in the chariot reserved for his second-in-command. And wherever Joseph went, the command was shouted, "Kneel down!" So Pharaoh put Joseph in charge of all Egypt. 44 And Pharaoh said to him, "I am Pharaoh, but no one will lift a hand or foot in the entire land of Egypt without your approval."

Week Three, Day 4

Question 2a (p. 53)

Daniel 2:12-19 *(NLT)*

[12] The king was furious when he heard this, and he ordered that all the wise men of Babylon be executed. [13] And because of the king's decree, men were sent to find and kill Daniel and his friends.

[14] When Arioch, the commander of the king's guard, came to kill them, Daniel handled the situation with wisdom and discretion. [15] He asked Arioch, "Why has the king issued such a harsh decree?" So Arioch told him all that had happened. [16] Daniel went at once to see the king and requested more time to tell the king what the dream meant.

[17] Then Daniel went home and told his friends Hananiah, Mishael, and Azariah what had happened. [18] He urged them to ask the God of heaven to show them his mercy by telling them the secret, so they would not be executed along with the other wise men of Babylon. [19] That night the secret was revealed to Daniel in a vision. Then Daniel praised the God of heaven.

Question 2b (p. 53)

Daniel 2:46-48 *(NLT)*

[46] "Then King Nebuchadnezzar threw himself down before Daniel and worshiped him, and he commanded his people to offer sacrifices and burn sweet incense before him. [47] The king said to Daniel, 'Truly, your God is the greatest of gods, the LORD over kings, a revealer of mysteries, for you have been able to reveal this secret.' [48] Then the king appointed Daniel to a high position and gave him many valuable gifts. He made Daniel ruler over the whole province of Babylon, as well as chief over all his wise men."

Week Four, Day 1

Question 3 (p. 65)

2 Samuel 6:12-23 *(NLT)*

12 Then King David was told, "The Lord has blessed Obed-edom's household and everything he has because of the Ark of God." So David went there and brought the Ark of God from the house of Obed-edom to the City of David with a great celebration. 13 After the men who were carrying the Ark of the Lord had gone six steps, David sacrificed a bull and a fattened calf. 14 And David danced before the Lord with all his might, wearing a priestly garment. 15 So David and all the people of Israel brought up the Ark of the Lord with shouts of joy and the blowing of rams' horns.

16 But as the Ark of the Lord entered the City of David, Michal, the daughter of Saul, looked down from her window. When she saw King David leaping and dancing before the Lord, she was filled with contempt for him.

17 They brought the Ark of the Lord and set it in its place inside the special tent David had prepared for it. And David sacrificed burnt offerings and peace offerings to the Lord. 18 When he had finished his sacrifices, David blessed the people in the name of the Lord of Heaven's Armies. 19 Then he gave to every Israelite man and woman in the crowd a loaf of bread, a cake of dates, and a cake of raisins. Then all the people returned to their homes.

20 When David returned home to bless his own family, Michal, the daughter of Saul, came out to meet him. She said in disgust, "How distinguished the king of Israel looked today, shamelessly exposing himself to the servant girls like any vulgar person might do!"

21 David retorted to Michal, "I was dancing before the Lord, who chose me above your father and all his family! He appointed me as the leader of Israel, the people of the Lord, so I celebrate before the Lord. 22 Yes, and I am willing to look even more foolish than this, even to be humiliated in my own eyes! But those servant girls you mentioned will indeed think I am distinguished!" 23 So Michal, the daughter of Saul, remained childless throughout her entire life.

Week Four, Day 2

Question 3 (p. 69)

Numbers 12:1-15 *(NLT)*

[1] While they were at Hazeroth, Miriam and Aaron criticized Moses because he had married a Cushite woman. [2] They said, "Has the Lord spoken only through Moses? Hasn't he spoken through us, too?" But the Lord heard them. [3] (Now Moses was very humble—more humble than any other person on earth.)

[4] So immediately the Lord called to Moses, Aaron, and Miriam and said, "Go out to the Tabernacle, all three of you!" So the three of them went to the Tabernacle. [5] Then the Lord descended in the pillar of cloud and stood at the entrance of the Tabernacle. "Aaron and Miriam!" he called, and they stepped forward. [6] And the Lord said to them, "Now listen to what I say:

> "If there were prophets among you,
>> I, the Lord, would reveal myself in visions.
>> I would speak to them in dreams.
> [7] But not with my servant Moses.
>> Of all my house, he is the one I trust.
> [8] I speak to him face to face,
>> clearly, and not in riddles!
>> He sees the Lord as he is.
> So why were you not afraid
>> to criticize my servant Moses?"

[9] The Lord was very angry with them, and he departed. [10] As the cloud moved from above the Tabernacle, there stood Miriam, her skin as white as snow from leprosy. When Aaron saw what had happened to her, [11] he cried out to Moses, "Oh, my master! Please don't punish us for this sin we have so foolishly committed. [12] Don't let her be like a stillborn baby, already decayed at birth."

[13] So Moses cried out to the Lord, "O God, I beg you, please heal her!"

[14] But the Lord said to Moses, "If her father had done nothing more than spit in her face, wouldn't she be defiled for seven days? So keep her outside the camp for seven days, and after that she may be accepted back."

[15] So Miriam was kept outside the camp for seven days, and the people waited until she was brought back before they traveled again.

Week Four, Day 3

Question 2 (p. 72)

Numbers 27:1-11 *(NLT)*

[1] One day a petition was presented by the daughters of Zelophehad—Mahlah, Noah, Hoglah, Milcah, and Tirzah. Their father, Zelophehad, was a descendant of Hepher son of Gilead, son of Makir, son of Manasseh, son of Joseph.
[2] These women stood before Moses, Eleazar the priest, the tribal leaders, and the entire community at the entrance of the Tabernacle. [3] "Our father died in the wilderness," they said. "He was not among Korah's followers, who rebelled against the Lord; he died because of his own sin. But he had no sons. [4] Why should the name of our father disappear from his clan just because he had no sons? Give us property along with the rest of our relatives."

[5] So Moses brought their case before the Lord. [6] And the Lord replied to Moses, [7] "The claim of the daughters of Zelophehad is legitimate. You must give them a grant of land along with their father's relatives. Assign them the property that would have been given to their father.

[8] "And give the following instructions to the people of Israel: If a man dies and has no son, then give his inheritance to his daughters. [9] And if he has no daughter either, transfer his inheritance to his brothers. [10] If he has no brothers, give his inheritance to his father's brothers. [11] But if his father has no brothers, give his inheritance to the nearest relative in his clan. This is a legal requirement for the people of Israel, just as the Lord commanded Moses."

Week Four, Day 3 (continued)

Question 2 (p. 72)

Numbers 36:1-12 *(NLT)*

[1] Then the heads of the clans of Gilead—descendants of Makir, son of Manasseh, son of Joseph—came to Moses and the family leaders of Israel with a petition. [2] They said, "Sir, the Lord instructed you to divide the land by sacred lot among the people of Israel. You were told by the Lord to give the grant of land owned by our brother Zelophehad to his daughters. [3] But if they marry men from another tribe, their grants of land will go with them to the tribe into which they marry. In this way, the total area of our tribal land will be reduced. [4] Then when the Year of Jubilee comes, their portion of land will be added to that of the new tribe, causing it to be lost forever to our ancestral tribe."

[5] So Moses gave the Israelites this command from the Lord: "The claim of the men of the tribe of Joseph is legitimate. [6] This is what the Lord commands concerning the daughters of Zelophehad: Let them marry anyone they like, as long as it is within their own ancestral tribe. [7] None of the territorial land may pass from tribe to tribe, for all the land given to each tribe must remain within the tribe to which it was first allotted. [8] The daughters throughout the tribes of Israel who are in line to inherit property must marry within their tribe, so that all the Israelites will keep their ancestral property. [9] No grant of land may pass from one tribe to another; each tribe of Israel must keep its allotted portion of land."

[10] The daughters of Zelophehad did as the Lord commanded Moses. [11] Mahlah, Tirzah, Hoglah, Milcah, and Noah all married cousins on their father's side. [12] They married into the clans of Manasseh son of Joseph. Thus, their inheritance of land remained within their ancestral tribe.

Download these *Free* PDFs from our website

Make business-card-size (2 x 3.5-inch) magnets for your group!

- Print this free downloadable artwork on cardstock, or semi-gloss or glossy brochure paper.

- Each PDF includes 12 images. The 3B Words are in bright pink lettering on a white background, and the Beauty words are in white lettering on a bright pink background. Cut into individual pieces (business-card size).

- Stick to business card magnets, available at your local office supply store.

- Or, you might want to laminate it as small bookmark, or frame it, or attach it to a keychain.

Shown in actual size: 2 x 3.5 inches

Shop Priority

Visit Priority's online store to find out more about Bible studies, DVDs, and CDs by Laurie Cole. Each product will encourage you to give God glory and priority.

Shop online now!
Monday - Friday, 9am - 4pm CST

www.priorityministries.org

There is a
Season
Bible Study
An 11-week study for women, designed to help you experience contentment in every season of life.

There is a **Season**

Experiencing Contentment in Every Season of Life

Laurie Cole

The Temple
Bible Study
Priority's *"you glo, girl"* 11-week Bible study will help you discover how to **glo**—glorify God.

The Temple

GLORIFYING GOD IN YOUR EVERYDAY LIFE

LAURIE COLE

Beauty by **THE BOOK**
Bible Studies

New!
FREE
Video Downloads
for both *Beauty by The Book* studies!

Beauty by THE BOOK

by Laurie Cole

Beauty by
The Book *for Teens*

Laurie Cole

Whether you're 17 or 70, learn the secrets of becoming a biblically beautiful woman.

Resources available for these studies:
Workbooks, Small Group CD-ROM Leader Guides, Video Lectures, and Audio Lectures.

Audio CD sets

Connect with Priority

Priority Partners

Priority Partners believe in the mission
of Priority Ministries and support it with
their generous financial gifts. Would you
prayerfully consider becoming a Partner and
helping us reach and teach women to give
God glory and priority in their lives?

Become a monthly or one-time donor. Either way, your financial gifts provide vital
support for this ministry! For more information about becoming a Priority Partner,
visit our website:

www.priorityministries.org

Priority *Blog*

Join our friendly ***Glo Girl*** community!
Our mission is to help you give God
glory and priority in your life.

Keep up with the latest Priority news,
and so much more!

Start off each week with Laurie's *Monday Manna* posts and end it with her
Front Porch Friday video teaching series. Continue your spiritual discipleship
with *Emily's Posts*, and take advantage of one of our *Online Studies*.

Have fun with our *Glo-ing at Home* posts, and download free *Scripture Art* for your
computer wallpaper or print it to encourage a friend.

We look forward to ***glo'ing*** with you!

www.priorityministries.org

Made in the USA
Middletown, DE
17 May 2021